Goodnight, Mary Ann

To Kie,
May you be inspired to
blaze new trails ...
Debra Stuffleberan
Dec, 2003

Goodnight, Mary Ann

❖

The LiveS of Mary Ann Sage

Debra Guiou Stufflebean

iUniverse, Inc.
New York Lincoln Shanghai

Goodnight, Mary Ann
The LiveS of Mary Ann Sage

iUniverse, Inc.

For information address:
iUniverse, Inc.
2021 Pine Lake Road, Suite 100
Lincoln, NE 68512
www.iuniverse.com

ISBN: 0-595-29476-6

Contents

Mary Ann Bassett Sage 1

Mary Ann Jones Dennitt Buell Sage 27

Epilogue 79

Genealogy 87

Bibliography 93

Favorite Historic Sage Inn Recipes 99

Mary Ann Bassett Sage

$\mathfrak{M}$y name is Mary Ann Bassett Sage. I was born August 19, 1832 in Glaston-bury, England to Joseph & Elizabeth Hale Bassett. I was the third child of nine children. Our family was friends with Samuel and Elizabeth Davis Sage, who lived in Somersetshire, England. My husband, Alfred Sage, who was born August 6, 1833, was the fourth child of nine that Samuel had with Elizabeth Davis. The nine Sage children were born at approximately the same time as the Bassett children were born.

Samuel Sage was the widower of Sharlot Hayden and they had four children: Charlotte, George, Aaron, and Mary Hannah. George married Mary Guppy in 1839 and moved to America in 1847. Alfred and his brothers, Arthur, John, and Mark couldn't wait to see this place that their half-brother wrote about. So in 1848 they began their voyage to America. Alfred was only 15 years old, but felt most certainly that he was a "man" up to the challenge. Mark, who was twelve, really had to beg to go with his older brothers.

My family and the rest of the Sage family came in 1849. It was not an uneventful voyage! We set sail on the *"Lucky Cosmore."* Strong winds blew us off course and we drifted clear down to St. Thomas Island. It took us three months and three days to finally reach New York. Water and food rations ran so low that it took its toll on my mother and baby brother. They died soon after our arrival in New York. I can't shake the memory of Willie, who was only four, with golden curls, and who loved to sing, begging for water with his little tin cup.

Our families settled in Skaneateles, New York. My older sister, Jane, and I resumed mother's responsibilities for caring for the younger children. But in 1854, at the age of 22, my papa gave permission for me to marry Alfred (age 21), and for my younger sister, Elizabeth (age 16) to marry John Sage (age 24). Alfred and I had courted for a while before he proposed. He was an adventurous one. He and John got it into their heads that they wanted to go West where they could own lots of land. Alfred told me he and John had spoken with their father about borrowing funds to travel West. It was a comfort to me to know that my sister would be with me to share the journey. Alfred and John signed a promissory note for $500 which they would repay as soon as they could afford to do so.

My little sister, Emma (age 13), ran off with Mr. Edwin Klintop who filled her head with silly notions about how much better her life would be married to him and moving to Iowa City. Papa was NOT pleased. I think she was jealous that Elizabeth and I were marrying and acted impulsively because upon her arrival in Iowa, we began receiving letters from poor Emma, who was terribly homesick and missed all of us dearly. Elizabeth and I convinced John and Alfred that we should join Emma and Edwin, as Emma had pleaded. The next I knew my brother, James, was planning to go, too! James (age 18) was a middle child in the family of Bassett children, number five of nine. He was four years younger than me, but two years older than Elizabeth. So in 1855, our small caravan set out for Iowa!

Emma was delighted to see us, although I'm not too sure how Edwin felt about suddenly having to house five other people. Things were very crowded, and we reassured Edwin that our move was only temporary until the men had jobs and money to purchase a place to live. Days turned into weeks, then months. I could tell that Alfred was getting impatient about having his own place. It would take time to afford land and be able to build a place for the five of us to live. Each couple had spent part of the $250 we had borrowed for wagons, horses, oxen and supplies. Alfred was reluctant to spend more without first building our nest egg back up.

Then one day in June of 1856, Alfred came home to get John. Told him to *"Hurry"* as there was someone in town that he wanted him to meet. That evening when the guys returned they were all fired up. Alfred had introduced John to General James Lane with the Kansas militia. Lane had ridden into Iowa to put together a party who would follow him back to Kansas. He reported that slave holders in Missouri were trying to tip the scales in their favor by stopping people from the North from taking the Missouri River into Kansas. I had heard about the tension in the Kansas territory. President Pierce signed the Kansas Nebraska Act in 1854 which gave settlers the right to choose whether Kansas would become a free state. Settlers would be allowed to put it to a vote. You may as well put a match to a powder keg. The bill gave incentive for people to keep others out who thought differently than themselves about slavery.

I admit that I wasn't excited about where things were headed. Only a couple of months earlier, I realized that I was with child. I hadn't told Alfred because I felt he had too much else to worry about. Lane reported to the newspapers that he had marked a trail with stone chimneys he had built leading the way from Iowa City, south to Mt. Pleasant, then across the state of Iowa west to Civil Bend. Any interested parties could follow the trail to Civil Bend, and have the assistance of a guide who would take them on into Kansas territory. Those who would make the journey would have plenty of cheap land to choose from; simply stake off the claim and go to the land office to pay $1.25 an acre. The government's Pre-emption Act of 1841 gave preferential treatment to squatters who could buy as much as 160 acres after having lived there six months. Naturally, Lane's intention once in Kansas was to recruit for his militia.

There were lively discussions in our household for days. When I finally told Alfred that I was with child, he seemed all the more determined to go to Kansas. It was the promise of land that was the driving force. Immediately he and John began making plans for going alone and sending for Elizabeth and I later. Just the idea of my husband going into a territory full of Indians and Bushwhackers terrified me, let alone him going without me and my not knowing where he was and what was happening. Sister and I agreed that if John and Alfred would not reconsider, then we would ALL go.

General Lane came to the Klintop house for dinner one evening at my husband's request. He was a very straight forward man who spelled out clearly the danger that lie ahead. Lane told us that the settlement of Lawrence had been sacked the month before by Bushwhackers. He reported that freedom hung in the balance and it was up to him to bring recruits to help John Brown and his sons fight off the ruffians. My Papa believed in abolition, as did Alfred's, but I could not believe that this was a cause that Alfred and John would be willing to risk their lives for. Lane was certainly passionate about recruiting for his militia, although I had doubts as to whether it was due to his concern for the slaves, or simply a desire to WIN in war. The men sat spellbound listening to Lane's carefully laid out plans.

James was equally enthused about going, but I pleaded with him to wait until we could directly size up the situation. I did not want to have my younger brother involved in all of this if I could prevent it. James finally relented and said he would stay *"a little longer"* with Emma and Edwin.

By the time we reached Civil Bend, July 4, 1856, we had picked up other wagons, including several at Mt. Pleasant which were loaded with weapons. I would have liked to have stayed in Red Oak, Iowa and left the wagon train, but Alfred was determined to go to Kansas. We spent a night at Tabor, then readied ourselves for crossing the Missouri River the following day, but to our surprise there was no bridge to cross over to Nebraska City. The crossing was a laborious operation, the men worked diligently, day after day, to get one wagon at a time across the river without dumping its contents. We had camps on both sides of the river.

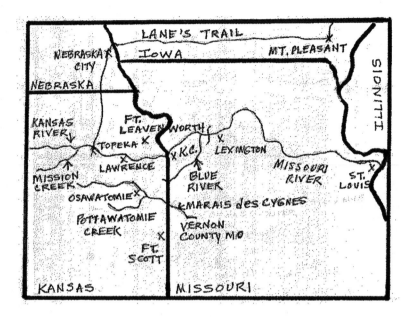

John Brown, himself, rode from Topeka, Kansas to meet with Lane. The camps spread with horror stories about Brown and his followers coming upon murdered abolitionists in Lawrence. Brown said they had no recourse but to take revenge for wrongs that had been done. After Brown reported that two of his sons, John Brown Jr. and Jason, had been captured and imprisoned at Camp Sackett, General Lane went crazy! Brown was overheard as saying, *"If the question of slavery cannot be handled by the ballot box, then I am ready and willing to handle it with the cartridge box!"*

John Brown had brought a Colonel Eldridge with him from Lawrence and suggested that they put him in charge of the wagon train, thus converting the wagon train's appearance of being an "invasion" to more of an "expedition." That way General Lane and John Brown, along with some of the rowdier young men, could make a hasty departure from the wagon train that night. The *"army"* was to continue due south. I was uncomfortable with our wagon train being referred to as an army. While some teams were loaded with arms and ammunition, most of us were peaceable people seeking homes in a new land. Those intent on being mercenaries, had ridden ahead.

We arrived in north Topeka along a military route that went from Ft. Leavenworth to Ft. Riley. It followed the Kansas River, but in order to cross the river, we had to take Pappan's ferry which was nothing more than logs tied together and rope pulleys used to move the platform across the river. Topeka was very flat and barren. The only bluff (or large mound) seen in the distance, I was told marked the country of the Pottawatomie who had a truly "big" chief, called Burnett, a friendly chap who was anxious to do horse trading with the white settlers.

Topeka wasn't as much of a town as I had thought it would be. There were very few buildings kind of sparsely dotting a road they called *"Kansas."* We were told we would be able to stay at the new Topeka House Hotel, but it was not yet finished, so we got a room at Chase's Boarding House instead. We actually got to see Chief Burnett one time as he was driven through town, riding in the back end of a wagon.

Only after we had arrived in Topeka, did I learn that Brown and his sons had hacked to death five pro-slavery settlers before he met with our camp. I wanted to tell Alfred and John, but they had already left our side to explore the area southwest of Topeka where folks said there was much unsettled land. They were told to go back to the military road and head west towards Indianola, near the Baptist Mission, where another ferry ran by Sidney Smith crossed the Kansas river and split off from the trail in a southerly direction. Elizabeth and I stayed in Topeka, partly because of my condition, but partly because I wanted to assess the political climate. How much did we really know about this John Brown? Citizens of Topeka seemed to admire him, but at the same time many were aghast at the news of what had transpired along Pottawatomie Creek.

I saw John Brown only one other time when he wished Elizabeth and I safe harbor in Kansas. He said he was leaving Kansas for a few days and I couldn't help wondering if he wasn't laying low until things sort of blew over. I never warmed to the man. There was something very eery about him, and he had eyes of steel.

John and Alfred reported wonderful news! The area southwest of Topeka along Mission Creek was as beautiful as the rolling green hillsides near Dover, England, our homeland. They said that along the creek, unlike the Kansas River, they found enough trees to build a cabin, and plenty native stone from which to build a more permanent structure later on. They dug a well until they hit upon an underground stream. When they drank from the creek water, they became ill and reported having intestinal pain. The creeks and streams were brimming from the previous winter's thaw and spring precipitation. The ground should produce plentiful crops.

I sent letters to James and Emma in Iowa, and also to our loved ones in New York. I reported on the beauty of the land, but also on the impending turmoil that some predicted would lead to war. Elizabeth and I were so joyful when Alfred and John returned to collect us. They teased us about how afraid we would be listening to the howl of wolves [coyotes] at night, and we teased right back that we weren't a couple of *"tenderfoots"* like them. Later even they confessed to being frightened their first night on the prairie. Neither got a wink of sleep. One kept watch from the front of the wagon with a gun; the other kept watch from the rear with an axe.

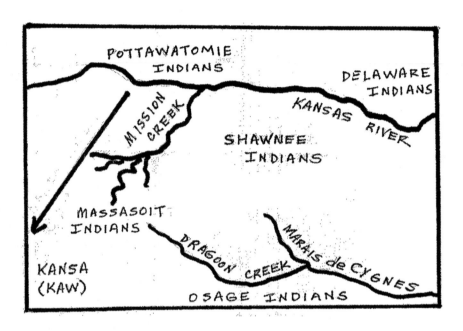

The Indians were worrisome to me. Only a couple of miles from our cabin was a tribe of Massasoit [3/4 mile southwest of where Massasoit Creek empties into Mission Creek]. We saw many Kansa Indians who went back and forth along this Southwest Trail from Council Grove to Topeka to draw money from the government. Previously they had a village along Mission Creek, then named American Chief's Creek, after their tribal leader. We were also in close vicinity to the Shawnee tribe at Brownsville [Auburn] and the Pottawatomie had a trading post and pay station north at Uniontown. The Indians were curious about the white settlers, but as long as *"the man"* was around, they kept their distance. Although no harm ever befell us, I never stopped being frightened of them. Too many stories from travelers passing through about Indians stealing women, be they true or not, reminded us to not let our guard down.

John Brown returned to Kansas, and I dreaded knowing that Alfred and John may be called to carry arms since they had promised to do so. That fateful night came when a member of the Kansas militia rode from Topeka to our small homestead. Carrying a note penned by Lane, himself, he requested that Alfred and John ride south with the courier to Council City [Burlingame] and make their way eastwardly to the banks of the Marais des Cygnes. General Lane had all available militia surrounding Lecompton, intending to rescue Dr. Robinson, a free state leader, from jail. At the same time, he was attempting to shore up support for Brown, whose family lived in Osawatomie.

Fortunately for Elizabeth and me, John and Alfred's first concern was for OUR safety. John, who at the time was ailing from a leg injury, decided to stay with us so we would not be alone in the wilderness. My heart sank, as I watched Alfred ride away. For several days, Alfred, and other men who joined along the way, rode to the aid of John Brown. Alfred narrowly escaped death, being young and inexperienced at war. They opened fire before Border Ruffians were within range and had difficulty controlling the horses who were skittish around the noisy firearms. The free-soilers were forced to retreat and watch while Osawatomie burned (Aug. 30, 1856). Brown, himself, was wounded, and his son, Fred, was killed.

A Connecticut preacher, Henry Ward Beecher, arranged to furnish General Lane's militia with Sharps rifles, which were superior to and more accurate than shotguns. Crates of rifles, covered with Bibles, were shipped to a church in Wabaunsee, Kansas. Lane could intercept the wagons enroute to Wabaunsee anytime after they were unloaded from the steamboat.

John Brown was at the height of his glory, giving fiery orations to the militia, encouraging them to keep calm and aim low. Praise God, the new territorial governor, John Geary, arrived from Lecompton accompanied by 300 U.S. Army dragoons. He negotiated a cease fire (Sept. 1856). The Missourians went home and the militia disbanded. John Brown rode to Nebraska City, narrowly escaping being captured. Dr. Robinson was released and free to return to Lawrence. Alfred returned to my waiting arms.

I was large with child that first fall (1856), and glad to have the Kansas summer over. Alfred and John began construction of a second log cabin that would be for Alfred and me. Our cabin measured 10' x 10' with a curtain strung on a rope down the middle. One side was used as a bedroom, the other side was for eating and fellowship. When the winter snow arrived, it sifted between the logs. It was freezing! We used a buffalo hide for warmth. We also learned to turn our shoes over at night so they wouldn't fill up with snow!

The letters I sent to New York describing our adventures, enticed Alfred's sister, Ann, her husband, Simon Main, and three children: Morris, Hester and

Frank, to come to Mission Creek. Simon's family had also immigrated from England. He and Ann had married before the rest of the Sage family had sailed for New York. Ann and Simon's baby son, Johnny, died soon after arriving in New York. The Mains arrived in Kansas in time for the birth of our first son, William Henry Bassett Sage. I wanted to name him after my baby brother who died when coming to America. To my surprise, Ann was about to conceive another child herself. Joe Main was born by the end of the year.

Jacob Haskell (age 54) and his son, Albert (age 22) homesteaded near to us. They had come from New Hampshire. Jacob's wife and other children remained back East until suitable lodging could be built. Before another winter, the men were determined to build two stone houses; the Haskell's would build one, the Sage's the other. The limestone could be mined along the creek, and it was a much superior source of protection from the Kansas winter.

I had a lot to be thankful for—my husband, my child, and the companionship of my sister and sister-in-law. Being without a church did not prevent us from setting aside time for prayer in each other's homes.

My foolish brother, James, could not wait out the long winter any longer. He was ready to leave Iowa and join all of us in Kansas. So in February, 1857, James headed to St. Louis to take a steamboat across the Missouri to Leavenworth. It was a slow and arduous journey of two weeks. Snags and sandbars slowed the speed of travel to a crawl. None of us knew James was coming, and we would have died worrying had we known he was attempting to make it to Kansas Territory via the Missouri River. Rev. Beecher's guns were discovered when a handyman opened one of the crates marked *"books."* Under the Bibles were found 25 Sharps rifles. From that point on steamboats were boarded in Lexington, Missouri and searched for contraband. James said everyone on board was a slave holder, or wouldn't profess to being anything other, nor would he for that matter. Thoroughly frustrated over the time it had taken him by boat, and not truly realizing the miles yet ahead from Leavenworth, James set out on foot. Fortunately my brother was strong and fit and had a broad smile that I am sure resulted in more than one lift along the way. James pre-empted his own claim, but took turns staying with either Elizabeth or I in our cabins. He rolled up his sleeves and started helping Alfred and John, and was also willing to help the Main's work their land.

That spring John, Alfred and James planted corn and sugar cane. We received so much rain that sugar cane got ten feet high and the corn shot to the sky! I made molasses from the sugar cane to eat on buckwheat pancakes (Yumm!). Food was plentiful: wild turkeys, turnips and mush. I seeded muskmelons, pumpkins, beans and squash in the garden. The vines grew like a jungle! John, Alfred, and the Haskells honed their skill at sawing limestone, and began laying foundations of two houses.

The Spring of 1857 also brought disease to Kansas: small pox killed many white settlers and Indians, alike. With so many travelers taking the Southwest Trail to connect with the Santa Fe Trail, it is truly a miracle that we escaped illness. People in Topeka were not as fortunate.

Many young bachelors came to Mission Creek to homestead: John and Noah Gibbs, William Collins, Jacob Orcutt, and T.D. Parks. An older couple, Daniel and Elizabeth Sayer, their daughter, Mary Ann, and two grandsons, James and Squire Dennitt settled on a neighboring claim. I became very fond of them. Daniel was an excellent stone mason from Pennsylvania and taught Alfred and others a great deal about masonry.

Alfred's younger brother, Mark, married Josephine Howe in New York; she had one son, Frank Howe. In July 1857, they decided to join our rapidly expanding Kansas family. Mark, being much stouter than his brothers and strong as an ox, said he would help build the stone house in exchange for lodging. Since the supplies we had started out with were close to being depleted, it was agreed that Mark and Josephine would purchase a wagon and some oxen in Iowa and bring a load of much needed supplies to us. I was very concerned about their safety, but Alfred said any man would think twice before trying to take on Mark Sage. The plan was that should they be stopped, Mark was to report his intentions to join Senator Atchison's army (pro-slavery).

Mark and Josephine drove from Iowa to Weston, Missouri where the wagon was put on a steamboat ferry. Ruffian inspectors satisfied themselves that nothing of a military nature was inside. Regardless of whether contraband was found, many passengers from the North were harassed, beaten, and even jailed. The crossing was without incident (Alfred must have been right), and they drove on to Leavenworth.

Mark read a poster in the Cody Hotel in Leavenworth that the government was looking for bullwhackers to freight grain to Denver and Taos. There was a limit to how much produce could be purchased by Topeka merchants. Without Topeka yet having a railroad or a steamboat, farmers had to drive their grain on to Leavenworth, or even Westport, to sell it all. Corn could be purchased for $1 a bushel in Leavenworth and sold for a $1 a pound in Denver and Taos. The government provided the wagons and the 16 oxen it took to pull each load. Each wagon needed two men, one to drive and one to lead the oxen. With one excursion under his belt, Mark saw this as an opportunity to help with the finances, and to set money aside for his own land. He recruited my brother, James, to be his partner. They would make trips to Leavenworth where they would sleep on the lobby floor of the Cody Hotel, until chosen to take a load. Mark and James made three trips to Taos and back between 1857 and 1861.

Jacob Haskell was pretty miserable without his wife, Mary Ann. He had not received a single letter since arriving in Mission Creek. I tried to comfort him that the mail to these parts was very unreliable. It was not on any regular schedule out of Leavenworth where letters were sent *"general delivery."* If someone going to Leavenworth just missed a letter, it could lay there several weeks before another would pick it up and bring it out to Mission Creek. Still I sympathized with the poor man, as we had been receiving mail from our relatives. I thought perhaps, I should make more of an effort to invite he and Albert over to eat with us.

Jacob Haskell hired some bare-bottomed Pottawatomies who didn't speak a bit of English! It was shocking to see them out and about lugging stones. Jacob would give a lot of hand gestures to direct their efforts. After a while they started saying, *"Come boys,"* because that was what Jacob used to tell them to get their attention. We were all anxious to see the stone houses completed, but it was taking much longer than anticipated.

News spread that John Brown was sited again in Kansas territory. He arrived bearded and using an alias and just as he had done before, he began recruiting men to follow him into battle. John and Alfred and a few of the other young men from the valley rode to meet with Brown who was hiding out on the Whitman farm near Lawrence. When it was realized that Brown was now wanting followers to go with him to Harper's Ferry, Virginia, they turned back. I'm sure Brown was very disappointed, maybe even angry when followers dropped in numbers. But by now our family had a few head of cattle, crops in the field, and only half of a stone house that needed completed before winter. I could tell that Alfred felt he had let John Brown down. He had become thoroughly sympathetic to the plight of the abolitionists, but I was relieved when he stayed behind. Little did I know that he had committed to assisting any runaway slaves who made it to Mission Creek.

As the days marched by, Jacob Haskell decided to abandon his efforts to get a stone house done before winter. Instead, he thought if he were to get Mary Ann and the children here before the first snow, he'd best put up a timber house. So he and Albert began sawing the timber to start building the house on Albert's claim next to the partially built stone house. He wrote to Mary Ann and told her of the change of plans, demanding that she give him some kind of answer so he would know whether to plan on returning home to get them or meeting them in

Leavenworth! At last the day arrived, joyously Jacob ran to tell others that he had received not one, but two letters from his daughters, Emma and Bette, who also made reference to an earlier letter sent by their mother. They would be accompanying Mr. Trickey to Kansas so there was no need for him to return to New Hampshire. Jacob and Albert would meet them in Leavenworth the end of October.

When the Haskell timber house was completed, with the help of the Indians, it was 16' x 22' with a breezeway down the middle. Alfred and his brothers liked the looks of it so much that they wondered if they couldn't make the top half of their stone house timber. So a vote was taken among us to do the top half of the house in timber. We would divide it in half for John and Elizabeth, who was pregnant with their first child, in one side; Alfred, Willie, and I in the other. James could live in John & Elizabeth's old cabin; Mark and Josephine could live in our old cabin until they found their own claim, and if the winter got bad, we'd make room for them in the *"big"* house.

There were good times in our new place. Alfred, John, Mark and James all got along so well. We wives could have all been sisters. Simon and Ann homesteaded right next to us so they were at our place as often as the rest of us. Some nights the fellas would take turns playing the harmonica which their father had taught them as young boys, and we would dance a reel. The children enjoyed it as much as we did, clapping their hands in delight to see their momma's and papa's having such fun. Rather than focus on our hardships, we thanked the Lord for the good times and the family around us.

I was so proud of my husband, and loved him dearly. He worked so hard, and yet always concerned himself with being sure that everyone else around him was also being taken care of. Alfred Sage was a very kind man. He would give the shirt off his back to a total stranger. I became better acquainted with the man I married, and to understand his motives for action, after he became a father. He was simply driven to become a man that his son could look up to, and to be able to leave a legacy to the family we would have together. Alfred felt that if he was not able to make something of himself, then all the sacrifices of his parents were for nothing. Alfred's father provided the means for all of us to head West; $500 was a lot of money for a man with mouths of his own to feed! Alfred would succeed, or die trying! More than anything, Alfred wanted to bring his aging father to Kansas, that he might see for himself the land, the growing crops, the cattle and yes, the name, that Alfred had made for himself.

My Alfred was well respected by others who turned to him for advice and assistance. He had a good head for business. I'm sure he would have become a successful business man had he chosen to remain back East. Already there was talk about developing a town, and when asked what we might call this new town, Alfred replied, *"Dover, America!"* For as far as we could see, the rolling Kansas Flint Hills were every bit as beautiful as the white cliffs of Dover, England. A dream, yes, but look at how far we had already come!

My brother James, as I had mentioned, made trips to Denver with Mark freighting grain. He didn't have the commitments of a family man, like Mark had, and in the Spring of 1858 when word around Denver spread like a grass fire that gold had been discovered in the Pikes Peak region, he told Mark that he was just going to stay on a bit and try his luck with mining. He told Mark he'd catch up with him on his next trip back to Denver.

Alfred's father, Samuel, did not come the next spring, but his next youngest brother, Samuel Jr. came. Alfred mailed letters to his father encouraging all of them to come, but Samuel felt it was too soon for all of them to come at once. It was a much better plan that as the boys got older, and another pair of hands was needed, Samuel would send them West to join us. He selflessly funded the wagon of supplies that would come as well. Our family did expand, though, in 1858. Ann gave birth to a baby girl, Ellen. Elizabeth and John had their first child, also a girl, Emma, who was named after our sister, Emma Klintop.

Samuel Jr. turned 19 the year he arrived, 1858. From the beginning, I could tell that he was less interested in homesteading than he was about getting involved in the looming conflicts of war. Immediately he joined the Kansas militia after hearing of five free-soilers being killed along the Marais des Cygnes. The massacre brought John Brown, himself, back to Kansas soil. Samuel said he saw Brown, but that he was very ill. He told Alfred that Brown was convalescing at his sister's, Florella Adair's, cabin in Osawatomie.

Then one night I overheard Alfred talking with Samuel outside our cabin. He told Samuel that he had secured some people who would be receptive to housing slaves if Brown really did try to take a group to Canada. He told him that Jehu and Mary Hodgson, who had a cabin on a trail south of us, would be willing to provide refuge, and Hodgson's were pretty sure that Henry & Ann Harvey would, also, but they'd have to use their attic. Alfred asked Samuel if he'd go about three miles west as the creek ran to the Beaches. He told Samuel that he had not met the Beaches who had came here in May. But those who had met them called Mr. Beach, *"Captain Beach,"* and said they came to Mission Creek from Canada. Alfred also thought he'd talk to Mary Ann Buell, the daughter of Daniel and Elizabeth Sayer. Mary Ann, a widow, had lost her husband to Border Ruffians over around Lawrence. From our friendship with her, he knew that she was a staunch supporter of abolition, besides Mary Ann and the Sayer's knew John Brown.

I was alarmed! Not only for Alfred, but for the safety of all of us. I told Alfred that I had overheard. He was upset that I had found out. He cautioned me that I mustn't say anything about it to any of the others because of the danger. I told him that was exactly why I couldn't believe he was going to provide shelter to slaves! He could get all of us killed! Alfred looked me squarely in the eyes, put his hands on my shoulders, and said, *"If I were Negro, would you want someone to help me?"*

I had never even given that a thought. I told him, *"of course,"* but I was also worried about Willie's safety.

Alfred said, *"You know I love you, Mary Ann. I would never do anything to jeopardize your safety, or Willie's. Don't you see? A man's got to do what he feels is right in his heart. I could not live with myself if I did not aid those slaves who are lucky enough to get this far on the road to freedom. They only need food and shelter for a short while as they make their way north, eventually to Canada. No man, woman or child should be owned by another."* And as he so valiantly pointed out, *"There but for the grace of God, go I!"*

Timing is everything. I chose that moment to tell Alfred that we would be having another child by late Spring. I never loved him more than I loved him that night, standing outside, alone, under the stars.

Winter set in and I felt certain that things would calm down due to the unpredictability of Kansas winters, but that turned out to be just what John Brown thought most people would think. Just a few days before Christmas, 1858, Brown led a raid with his followers into Vernon County, Missouri, east of Fort Scott. Eleven Negroes were freed from the Hicklin and Cruise farms. Cruise resisted and was killed. Brown fled with the Negroes along the Pottawatomie Creek southeast of us, so I knew that he would be working his way northwest, perhaps even to Mission Creek.

Alfred was gone more than he was home that month. Days would go by without my seeing him, but I didn't ask. If someone asked of the whereabouts of Alfred, I would tell them that he was in Topeka on business, or that he was helping Mark move a load of corn west for the winter. Never was a word spoken about Brown's activity in the area.

In early February, 1859, after Alfred had been gone for nearly two weeks, he returned to tell me it was finished. He reported that in a skirmish north of Holton, Brown and the slaves had nearly been captured. Several free-soilers from Topeka rode to hold the Bushwhackers at bay. Brown gave the order for the

Negroes to continue north to a place known as *"Pony Creek,"* there they would find a cave and be entering Nebraska. We never discussed where Alfred had gone, or even if he had harbored slaves close by. That Spring, I gave birth to another baby boy, Squire J. Sage.

Mark brought back a weary brother, mine, from Denver his first trip of the Spring in 1859. Grinning like a Cheshire cat, that Bassett smile, he opened his knapsack and brought out three little pouches. He said, *"Now don't open these until I tell you to."* He handed one to Elizabeth, one to me, and tossed one at Mark, *"Here you go, par-d-ner!"* he said teasingly. The suspense was killing us. *"Ok,"* and we quickly began untieing the pouch we'd been given. Each held a handful of sparkly nuggets.

"Gold!" Elizabeth exclaimed.

"Very funny, James" John remarked. *"It's fools gold, isn't it?!"*

"Nope, dear brother-and-law, I struck the REAL thing. This here's my gift to all of you for putting up with me."

"What do they think the claim may be worth?" Alfred asked.

"Well, lets just say we've mined $100,000 so far!"

For most of 1859, James Bassett was in the Pike's Peak region. The boon was over almost as fast as it had started. But, before his claim went bust, it yielded one-half million dollars! He returned to Kansas with Mark, his last trip before snow would make the trail impassable.

As the year had worn on, we went from a normal spring to a dry summer, to drought by fall. As the climate changed in Kansas, settlers went back to from wherever they had come. Only the strong endured. Land was passed around among those who did stay. Some stayed with their original claim, others used it to negotiate for another parcel to see if they'd have better luck with that piece of land.

The next time we heard of John Brown was in a letter from Alfred's brother, Aaron (age 18) in December, 1859. Alfred read the letter aloud to all of the family as we gathered in our cabin that night. Even Mark, Samuel, and my brother, James, were home at the time. The letter read:

Christmas, 1859—

Dear brothers, John, Alfred, Mark, and Samuel, and my sister, Ann—

Greetings and Merry Christmas! It seems everywhere I read about the unrest in Kansas and to think my adventuresome family is smack in the middle of the controversy! I feel certain that we are destined for Civil War. John Brown attempted a raid on Harper's Ferry in Virginia mid-October—a bloody massacre—that resulted in the death of many Kansas raiders and the capture of Brown, himself. Knowing your true feelings in the matter, I anxiously read the names of those involved. I followed Brown's trial in the newspapers, and while it is doubtful that you do not know this, I bring you news of John Brown's death by hanging. What's more, four other raiders were also hanged: Copeland, Green, Coppoc and Cook. I feel torn between wanting to be involved in your courageous cause, and my allegiance to father and mother. Mother, sadly, is not a bit well. I fear she grows frail. I promise you this, dear brothers, that should we go to war, Walter and I will wait no more. We will enlist and do our duty from this part of the country.

I received Mary's note, so congratulations, Alfred and Mary, on the birth of your second son. These boys will help you develop a prosperous homestead in your beloved Kansas. Walter asks that he be remembered to all. Father and mother send their love, as do I. Aaron

I thought about how close we came to one of those raiders being Alfred. My feelings were mixed about John Brown's death. On the one hand, I knew that the cause to free slaves was like a snowball rolling down a hillside, picking up speed and growing larger. On the other, I was not convinced that the ways of John Brown were good for those who believed in him. I feared he felt all were dispensable, including himself, if slavery were abolished in the end. When people are so zealous they can become reckless in their regard for life. Indeed, his outcome was inevitable. Our Christmas was void of celebration after Aaron's letter. The men seemed dazed, and the women worked silently preparing food and keeping the little ones occupied.

Alfred and Samuel journeyed back to New York to see their mother in April, 1860. John and Mark stayed behind as both Elizabeth and Josephine were expecting babies. Ann, too, was with child. As the drought continued, we knew we'd become short on both food and supplies. They would be able to replenish some of our needs by bringing a wagon back. It was hard to believe that we lived in the same Kansas from even a year ago. The land was so hard, you couldn't get a plow to penetrate it.

Alfred had an opportunity while in New York to call upon his cousin, Russell Sage, an influential member of the U.S. House of Representatives, who was very interested in how life was going in the territory. Russell was a very eloquent speaker in the House in support of abolition. Alfred was always very proud when he would read something written in the newspaper of his cousin's performance:

"Mr. Chairman, the people of Kansas, thus oppressed and subjugated, have appealed to Congress for relief; they have complained and struggled in vain. The free state people have done as the people of the territory of Michigan and California had done before them: that is, formed a state constitution that invites ALL people to par-

ticipate therein, but all such attempts have but brought down on them the reproach of being traitors, and subverters of authority!" Once again, the people of Kansas were making an impassioned plea—FOOD—PLEASE.

Alfred and Samuel knew that it would be the last time for either of them to see their mother. Before Alfred and Samuel had returned, a new Alfred and Samuel had been born. Ann and Simon had a son, Alfred Main; John and Elizabeth had a son, Samuel Sage.

Our crops were devastated that summer. In eleven months we had received only four inches of rain. We got one bushel of corn per acre, whereas in better years, our land might yield 50 or more bushels per acre. After two consecutive years of showing nothing for their labor, Alfred and John decided that they would try their hand at raising sheep instead of growing crops. My poor sister-in-law, Josephine, struggled with the heat as she carried Mark's first baby. Jennie Sage was born late in the summer.

The Legislature of the state of New York, appropriated $50,000 for disaster relief in the Kansas territory. Every free state in the union, also gave generous donations of money and goods. Samuel Pomeroy was appointed distribution agent for the territory. Alfred and John decided that our old cabin would be ideal for a store where they good distribute assistance in our immediate area. The cabin was built close to the trail, and was sitting empty now that Mark had finished building he and Josephine's house on land northwest of us.

John and Alfred could take turns driving to Leavenworth and signing for the government subsidy and bring it to the store for persons to pick up. When things turned around, people could stock the store whenever there was a surplus, and John and Alfred could keep track of the barter and charge business. What's more, mail could be delivered to the store and be picked up by those living "up" Mission Creek, while Harvey Loomis handled mail for those who lived "down" Mission Creek.

Father Lewis St. John and his wife, Sara, and sons, John and Mark, came to Mission Creek in 1860 in the middle of the drought. Lewis was not a farmer and everyone called him *"Father"* as he devoted his life to establishing worship centers in the Indian territories. At the age of 50, Lewis was hard of hearing and used a brass ear trumpet to hear. He was a kind soul. I was amused at how quickly young Mark (13) got a crush on one of the Haskell twins, Bette, who was several years older than him. Later that year, John St. John sent for his sweetheart, Frances Johnson, to join him. They were married by Jacob Haskell who was our new Justice of the Peace. We thought it would be a good idea to have someone to act as mediator in the event of disputes between neighbors. Jacob was a fair man and very logical, which made him a good choice.

W. A. Eddy and his wife, Harriet Blodgett Eddy, also came in 1860 from Grand Ledge, Michigan. "Washington" and Harriet had one son, Israel who was 15 years old.

We were prepared for the news that Alfred's mother had died that summer. Nothing could have prepared us for the devastation that followed the news. Simon and Ann's two little girls, Hester and Ellen, came down with high fever and coughing [diphtheria]; then John and Elizabeth's little girl, Emma, started having the same symptoms and gasped for air as though her throat was closing up on her. We immediately tried to quarantine the children from each other. Two of Ann's boys, Frank and Alfred, also came down with it. Before the scourge had left our homes, the baby girls had died, Ellen and Emma. A few days later, it took Hester who was eight. We had hoped that she would pull through it as her brothers did, but she did not.

When Josephine and Mark's baby, Jennie, was born, I honestly don't know if all the tears were from joy or mourning the loss of our other little girls.

Abraham Lincoln was elected to be our new president on Nov. 6, 1860. He did not receive even one vote in ten of the southern states. The following month South Carolina seceded from the United States. In January, Mississippi, Florida, Alabama, Georgia, Louisiana and Texas followed suit. I gave birth to another son, James, on the day that Kansas was admitted to the Union of the United States on January 21, 1861. His birth was almost overshadowed by the cloud hanging over our country.

Upon taking office in March, Lincoln appealed to the country to *"not break our bonds of affection,"* but in April a cannon was shot at Ft. Sumter in Charleston, South Carolina. The battle lasted 34 hours. On April 13, 1861, President Lincoln called his military to arms. Angrily refusing to bear arms against the southern states, Virginia, North Carolina, Tennessee, and Arkansas then also seceded.

My brother, James Bassett; Alfred's brother, Samuel Jr.; Squire and James Dennitt, Mary Ann Buell's sons, were among the first to respond. All belonged to Company F, 2nd Kansas U.S. Voluntary Cavalry. Some members of the second regiment were sent to Washington D.C. to serve as the frontier guards for President Lincoln. William Ross and Chester Thomas were among those who bivouacked in the White House.

Robert E. Lee, who guided the men in capturing John Brown at Harper's Ferry, VA, was offered General-in-Chief of the Union army. He declined, unwilling to turn against his home state of Virginia. Brig. General Irvin McDowell was appointed instead. McDowell and troops attempted to cross from Washington to Richmond, 100 miles south, which had been chosen as the new capitol of the confederacy (July, 1861). They encountered rebels under the command of General Beauregard and were defeated. McDowell was then replaced by Major General George B. McClellan who took command of troops again in Washington.

President Lincoln proclaimed blockades at all southern ports. I later learned that the navy only had three men-of-war on the east coast. The Union rapidly set into motion construction and recommission of ships. This was great news for Aaron and Walter who had enlisted in December and wanted to have a role in fighting the battle on sea, rather than land. We received a letter from Aaron, Christmas, 1861, saying that in October the mightiest armada ever assembled in the United States, set sail for Port Royal Sound between Charleston and Savannah. Seventy-five ships, 169 guns, 12,653 soldiers, 1,500 horses and stores of ammunition headed for Fort Walker. Aaron was in training to become a cannoneer on a battleship. Remembering that their father, Samuel Sage, had fought for the British when Napoleon threatened to conquer the world, he told us that Major General McClellan had earned the nickname of *"Little Napoleon."*

Closer to home, Captain Nathaniel Lyon was successful in capturing St. Louis for the Union, but as he proceeded westward in Missouri, he encountered Major General Sterling Price at Springfield. The Union soldiers retreated after Lyon was killed. We were greatly concerned about Price's activity in Missouri because we knew ultimately that the Kansas militia may be headed for conflict should Price attempt to cross into Kansas.

The stagecoach went from Leavenworth to Topeka, then southwest to Mission Creek. It forded where the banks shallowed out enough to get wagons and horses acrossed it [behind the Dover Cafe]. The John Copp family lived six to eight miles west on the stage route to Council Grove where Mission Creek tributaries originate [in Mill Creek township, approximately ten miles south of Paxico; closest town was "Halifax" (later changed name to Hessdale)]. He paid Mark to build a stone house/lay-over stage station since by the time the stage left Topeka, it was nightfall in the valley [thought to be on North Branch Road, first road south off of Skyline Drive]. While money was scarce among the locals, news of gold being found in Nevada brought increased traffic, newcomers chasing their dreams of striking it rich.

We were all happy for Ann and Simon when they had a new little girl, Libby, born in the Spring of 1862.

Company F of the Second Cavalry of the Kansas Militia was sent to northern Arkansas under orders of General S.R. Curtis. In March, 1862, we received a letter from my brother, Lieutenant Colonel James Bassett, that he had been engaged in battle with the confederates at Pea Ridge. He said for over three days he was embattled with rebel soldiers that included war-whooping Indians. Many fought with tomahawks, bows and arrows and war clubs.

"I narrowly missed a tomahawk that grounded in a ledge behind where I stood, which caused a piece of flint to ricochet from the blade and into my eye. I fear I may be getting an infection, and have not been able to see from it since the incident." They were successful in breaking up the confederate concentration in Arkansas, depriving the Rebels of easy access to Missouri.

We were appreciative that Aaron, too, was so good about writing. Since he and Walter continued in the same military unit, the only news from Walter was a post script to letters Aaron mailed. Aaron had become a number one gunner assigned to Major General A. E. Burnside. President Lincoln was anxious for a victory. General McClellan had not moved the forces for months while in the meantime the confederates sunk two of the Fed's steam frigates. Burnside held the bridge at Whitehall and the Federals took Roanoke Island in February. A month later they captured the seaport of Newbern, North Carolina and expeditions were sent out to Plymouth and Washington, N.C.

Walter stayed behind at Newbern after becoming very ill. When Aaron returned, he found Walter so weak that he pulled sentry duty for him. Unfortunately my brother-in-law, who was trying to handle Walters duties as well as his own, fell asleep while on guard. Aaron was jailed, court marshaled and sentenced to death. Now Aaron was a very well-liked young man. It is still a mystery to me how word eventually reached President Lincoln's ears, but Lincoln intervened saying that *"any soldier who would do duty for a sick brother or comrade, was not to be taken as he was too valuable to be lost."*

Only a few days before, we had received the letter from Aaron, so we were surprised to receive another letter so soon. It was simply addressed to *"The Sage Family,"* but when we opened it we found it was a letter from Alfred's father, Samuel, not Aaron.

March 30, 1862.

"Loved ones. My grief is almost too much to bear. The grim reaper has plucked another member of our family from among us. Walter, who was stationed at New Bern, N.C., contracted typhoid fever. I have received notice, just today, of his death. Father"

We were in shock. Alfred was sober and still for a while, then he said, *"I just remembered something old John Brown once said, 'Take more care to end life well, than to live long.' My brother died serving his country."*

Mail from troops was not always timely. We worried about how Aaron was handling Walter's death. Poor Walter. He was so young and would never set foot on Kansas soil.

I believe when God taketh away, he sends a soul to replace it. My sadness for Walter was replaced with gladness as I gave birth to our first daughter! Jokingly I reported that after three boys, it was about time that I got some help in the kitchen. We named her Margaret, and called her *"Maggie."* She was beautiful. Everyone said she looked just like me, but I thought she was much prettier.

Several months passed before we heard anything from Aaron. I feared that something must have been wrong with him, as well. It was not like Aaron to not write, particularly since he knew we would be anxious to hear the details of Walter's death. When his letter arrived, it began with an apology.

"Dear ones, you must forgive me for not writing. I, too, have been ill with typhoid fever. About the same time that Walter died, I was sent to fight at Fort Macon on Cape Lookout in North Carolina. With its capture, the Federals now control most of the North Carolina coastal waterway. I was not with Walter when he passed away so I am unable to give any details, and I could not bring myself to even write about it as my grief hit me hard. Walter and I have shared a lot in the short time that we served together. The conditions in which we serve are inhumane, scant food and filth, causing disease to run rampant. Our ship was sent to Jacksonville, Florida where we will stay through Christmas, in the hopes that the ill will recover, and those that don't, can be laid to rest.

My violin has kept me company. In fact, after others learned of my talent, I was asked to play for a dance, but this nearly put me in hot water again! One of the officer's lady friends took a fancy to my playin' and every opportunity would come over to sit by me to watch me play. The officer became so jealous that the dance was broken up and the ladies were asked to leave. I thought for sure that I was on my way to the stockade! You may try to get a letter to me at the address on the envelope. I am anxious to hear how the family is doing in Kansas, but the U.S. mail may not prevail. Love, Aaron

P. S. An officer asked me recently if Henry Valentine Sage from New York was any relation. Henry has apparently enlisted and is stationed in New York. His name stood out because he remembered "Valentine." I told him he was my nephew, our half-brother, George's, son.

Perhaps I spend too much time being preoccupied with the weather, but living in Kansas is not for the faint of heart. The weather is so extreme that it is either dry, blowing dirt and grit in your hair and eyes, or a blizzard, with snow so deep you can't get the front door open. I've seen ice break the bough of the strongest trees. Thunder clouds can promise rain and produce nothing more than lightening that boomerangs from the sky, touching the ground and reverting back. If the weather has been dry, the lightening ignites the prairie grasses. Acres and acres burn and a fog of smoke settles in the valley. If it does rain, it rains so hard and fast, the ground can't absorb it, causing flooding and erosion.

We had limited success at raising alfalfa hay for our livestock, also selling or trading it to others for their livestock. Cows gave us milk. I spun the wool from our sheep and sold it as a commodity in our store.

My prayers for Elizabeth were answered when Maddie was born. Our two little girls, Maggie and Maddie, would grow up together and be close, just as Elizabeth and I were.

I enjoyed the company of Fannie Ross who occasionally came into our store. Her husband, Edmund, and his brothers, William and George had bought land west of us in Wabaunsee County. We had first met in Iowa City as they were one of the families who decided to go to Kansas on the Lane Trail. She told me they had come down the Janesville Plank Road from Milwaukee, where the Ross's had run a newspaper. Their political views had led to the paper's financial demise; they were migrating to a place where they could *"make a difference."* Indeed, as soon as we got to Topeka, the Ross's set out for Lawrence where they bought the *Kansas Tribune*. Before the year was over, the Ross's closed the Lawrence paper and relocated in Constitution Hall in Topeka, after being repeatedly harassed by Sheriff Samuel Jones who was pro-slavery. The newspaper became the *Topeka Tribune*, then the *Kansas State Record* in 1859. Largely due to the political savvy of Edmund G. Ross and his paper, Topeka was selected as our state capital. He helped to raise campaign funds that resulted in Topeka being chosen as the state capital by voters on November 5, 1861.

After President Lincoln was elected, and it became evident that state's were seceding from the Union, the Ross's sold their interest in the newspaper in order to serve their country; but only after encouraging other free-soilers to *"fight as the children of Israel marched out of Egypt to the promised land!"* Fannie was more knowledgeable about the Civil War than I. Edmund became a Major under General Blunt, who had taken command over troops in Arkansas. In December, 1862, Edmund led the 11th Kansas Cavalry during a battle at Prairie Grove, successfully driving back over 11,000 confederates. They pursued them to Fort Smith where the rebels tried to reorganize but the Cavalry kept coming, driving them to Little Rock before the Rebels finally retreated. You could tell her stories were given to her by a newspaper man! I felt captivated, not only because James and Samuel were serving the Cavalry in Arkansas, but because Fannie knew so many details.

In January, 1863, the Homestead Act of 1862 was officially put into effect which brought many new settlers to our area. Land was free to heads of households who were 21 years of age or older and a U.S. citizen. A filing fee of $10 was all that was required to homestead 160 acres. After living on the land for five years, the owner received the deed. Alfred went with Mark to the land office where Alfred paid the claim for Samuel in order for him to have land near to us. The claim would be north of the Sayer's place.

Mark had previously bought 90 acres and was living west of Mission Creek. However, he wanted to buy 160 acres further west nearer to Copp's stage station where he worked part of the time. He built a fine home with his signature arches for doors on each end, east and west, tall rectangular windows on the second floor, and gun port windows near to the ground.

Over night the valley filled up with new people, which brought a boon to our store. Alfred decided to build a saw/grist mill. New housing would be needed and he could mill the logs and lumber for the cabins. He also would work out an arrangement to be paid in bushels of grain in exchange for milling services. Between the land being populated with livestock, the store, and now building of a mill, things were looking more prosperous. Mark and Josephine had their second daughter, Ida, and I became pregnant with our fifth child, which should be due around Christmas time.

I told Alfred that we women were concerned about the children having schooling. I had heard from Mr. Smith at the ferry crossing that his daughter, Isabel, might be interested in teaching school. I wondered if Alfred would have any objections if we turned our old cabin into a school house for the children? He thought it was a grand idea, so Elizabeth and I drove to the Smiths to make the offer. Shortly after Isabel began teaching for us, she was exchanging marriage vows with Thomas Haskell.

Major Ross was directed by General Ewing to take two companies to Lawrence, Kansas and set up camp on the west hill. There was concern about possible guerrilla raids on the city, but within a short time the citizens petitioned General Ewing to move the soldiers who were making too much noise while being on stand-by. General Ewing acquiesced and moved the troops to a point in western Missouri.

On August 20, 1863 a gang of raiders led by William Quantrill crossed the Kansas River near Aubrey. Fifty miles later, they waited for dawn. One hundred fifty persons were killed in Lawrence on August 21st. Major Ross and his troops were immediately dispatched to Lawrence, but it was too late. The following month, General Ewing warned Topeka that an encore performance may be in the works for Topeka, but fortunately this did not happen.

We received a letter from Aaron that they had attacked Charleston, which was second only in importance to Richmond. Under Admiral Dahlgren and General Quincy Gilmore, eight monitors moved within range of Fort Wagner, on the tip of Morris Island. Aaron's ship, *New Ironsides,* received as many as 60 hits in a day but Admiral Dahlgren knew precisely at what distance to place a monitor so that their ironclad armor would not be penetrated. For days, Fort Wagner was shelled by the monitors. Meanwhile Gilmore succeeded in setting up a cannon in the swamp to the rear of the island. The soldiers called the cannon, "The Swamp Angel." After Fort Wagner was evacuated, they began shelling Fort Sumter. Sumter had five lines of torpedoes that were impenetrable.

Aaron's letter read, *"I saw something like a cigar coming toward us, the next moment the ship was laid nearly on her beam-ends by the explosion. It didn't sink ol' Ironsides, but we retreated. But, I might add only after leaving much of the fort in rubble! I continue to think of all of you often. It is lonely being separated, and I miss Walter more than you'll ever know. I shall continue to patrol the seas. Blockade running is big business! When night falls, you must really be on guard. There are no search lights on these ships, so they're almost on top of you before you know they're out there! My love to all of you. Aaron"*

I kept thinking that I was going to have a Christmas baby. The days were counting closer, but the baby had not turned. I worried that this far along in my pregnancy, it may be a breach birth. My sister and sister-in-laws tried to keep me from worrying, but I was in terrible discomfort and the baby was very active! My sister-in-law, Ann, who had given birth many times, had also helped midwife some of the other babies. She said, *"If need be, I'll just reach up there and turn that child. I've pulled calves from many a cow!"* Of course we all got a good chuckle as her face turned beet red, realizing that what she had said would have offended most women.

On December 19, 1863, Thomas Dudley Sage was born in the middle of the night in our little cabin. I woke up when my water broke in bed; Alfred went to get Ann. When Ann arrived she could see a tiny blue foot. She attempted to re-arrange Thomas but since the birth was dry and the baby was large, had no choice but to pull to get him to come out. The pain was unbearable as she tore him from me. His one leg was dislocated and Ann worked with him a long time to get him to breathe. Meanwhile, I was losing a lot of blood. She screamed for Alfred, who was keeping the other children behind the curtain, to come assist her. She handed him his son, umbilical cord still attached, and told him to use the knife on the table to cut it while she got more rags for blotting so she could see what needed to be done.

I was so weak, sweat was beaded on my forehead, my hair was drenched. Ann told Alfred to get more blankets. I heard her say, *"She's going into shock."* Alfred laid more blankets on me. I could see from his face that he was frightened.

I mumbled, in and out of consciousness, *"What's happening?"* Alfred laid the baby in a basket by the bed and knelt down beside me. He kissed my forehead.

"Don't worry, Mary Ann, it'll be OK. Just rest. Go to sleep." I closed my eyes and let myself slip under, as Alfred whispered, *"Goodnight, Mary Ann."*

Mary Ann Jones Dennitt
Buell Sage

My name is Mary Ann Jones Dennitt Buell Sage. I was born to English Quaker parents in Bedford County, Pennsylvania, January 17, 1818. My parents were Isaiah and Elizabeth Jones. My grandparents told me we were from the William Penn colony of Philadelphia. They used to tell me stories of colonial days in America. *"Philadelphia"* means *"city of brotherly love,"* and they said I should always be proud of being a Quaker. Quakers have respect and compassion for all human beings. They made friends with the Indians and were one of the first colonies to emancipate slaves, as they felt having slaves was inconsistent with their religious doctrine.

My father died when I was a young girl. My mother married Daniel Sayer and they moved across the Allegheny Mountains to Erie, Pennsylvania, settling along Conneaut Lake. My step-father was a brick mason. He was proud of his building skills and his talent was always in demand. Brick was often shipped on barges down the Ohio River, which runs through my home state. Many homes along the river's edge were made by masons like him. He used to tell my mother, *"With these hands, I can get a job anywhere!"*

When I was 21 years old, I married a Quaker friend, Ephram H. Dennitt and moved to Ohio. The next year, I gave birth to my first son, James C. Dennitt (1840). Before another year had passed, we had a second son, Squire (1841). For reasons that shall remain between my husband and myself, I left Ephram five years later, and took my sons to live with my parents in Erie. There I filed for a divorce. I met Lucian Sheldon Buell, a young good looking lawyer who had moved from Connecticut to Erie, Pennsylvania to practice law. He was three years older than me, and the attraction was undeniable. He became my second husband in 1850.

Almost from the beginning, I realized that I had made a mistake. I had married outside of the Quaker faith, without realizing how much of who I had become was aligned with those principles. For instance, Lucian and I held very different views about slavery. He was from a wealthy family, and had grandparents in Virginia that owned several Negroes. I was always anxious to speak my political views, whereas he was more conservative for fear that it may affect his law practice. Ironically, in time it was my view point that was the more popular. I know that I was far too assertive for a woman of my time, and Lucian did not like that. When the New England newspapers started writing articles about taking colonies West, I was exhilarated just thinking of the prospect. Lucian was not. My marriage was never accepted by the Quaker order, who didn't believe in divorce. I decided to take my sons and flee from Erie. I would go to the opposite corner of the state, to Philadelphia, where my grandparents had lived. There I would again use the name Dennitt. If Lucian wanted a divorce, then he'd have to petition for one.

Naturally, a few years later, when Lucian was ready to re-marry, he did just that. He filed for divorce on the grounds of desertion. The petition was published, and my parents were mortified.

In the meantime, I worked as a cook in Philadelphia. I took care of my boys, and saved money, because when Eli Thayer, who wrote of his *"experiment"* in all the New England newspapers, was ready to put it to the test, I wanted to go; a new beginning in a new land. I was in contact with my parents by letter and after they experienced *"much to do about nothing,"* Daniel and Elizabeth Sayer joined me in Philadelphia. It was never my intentions to disgrace them, not that they ever said that I did, but I knew they were upset with me. At the same time, I knew they loved me. My dad was a good man. Good to my mother. Good to me and my boys. He always took things a day at a time. Said he could build houses in Philadelphia, same as in Erie!

Ephram Dennitt's family had shared the news of my scandalous divorce with him, too! A letter from Ephram was forwarded from my parents old address. It was originally post marked Boston, Massachusetts. Ephram told me he still loved me, and regretted dearly mistakes made in the past. He wanted to be a father to his sons and asked if there was any hope of reconciliation. I knew I had not loved Lucian. It was a whirlwind romance that ended after the infatuation had passed. I didn't know for sure how I felt about Ephram, but I did love my sons. I promised to give it some thought.

All the newspapers were ablaze with news of the passage of the Kansas Nebraska Bill, May 30, 1854. Settlers in Kansas would be given the opportunity to decide for themselves whether the state would become free! Horace Greeley of the widely read *New York Tribune* was a supporter of Eli Thayer's, promoting the plan to transplant a New England colony to Kansas. Thayer formed the Massachusetts Aid Society and sold shares of stock in the company in order to raise capital to buy land and supplies for his great adventure. The value of the land should increase rapidly upon the construction of a town.

When the time came near, a Boston newspaper reporter, S. F. Tappan, wrote an announcement that the Massachusetts Aid Society would be leaving from

Worcester train depot on July 17, 1854. *"The train will make the following stops: Albany, Buffalo, Erie, Detroit, Chicago, Alton and St. Louis. There, passengers will board a steamboat to Kansas City. The fare is $25 per person, the Society will pay the other half. Meals are extra. Adults are allowed to take 100 pounds of baggage. Upon arrival in Kansas, food and shelter will be available at the lowest prices as a result of the Society having already purchased many acres of land. The colony will include persons who can provide mechanical instruction and training. The first order of business will be to erect a press, school, and church."*

I made my decision. I told my parents that I was taking the boys to Kansas. We would be waiting at the depot to make the excursion. Full of sadness and remorse, they agreed to take us to Massachusetts. I wrote a letter to Ephram and gave it to my mother with instructions to mail.

When the day arrived, there was much festivity at the train depot. People were waving flags and singing. In a short time we all had the words down,

"We cross the prairies, as of old
the Pilgrims crossed the sea,
to make the West, as they the East,
the homestead of the FREE!"

I was amazed at the number of persons who showed up, as was Eli Thayer. While several men had been pre-selected to make the trip, I assumed that women would be needed to. I was a good cook, and a strong woman.

I met Dr. Charles Robinson who would be the agent accompanying the colony. Census information was given to a scribe at the depot. I was asked for the name of my husband, after seeing me with James and Squire, ages 13 and 15. I was certain there would be no problem. Boys younger than my sons had been known to journey west—alone! But, when the list was called out, we were not included. We were told that another group would be joining this colony in one month, perhaps we would be able to go then. My heart sunk.

My parents could tell how deeply despaired I was to not be included in the group that departed. I sat silently in the wagon as we left the city and prepared for the journey back to Philadelphia. My father, Daniel Sayer, broke the silence. *"You know, mother, I can make a living with these hands anywhere. Seems like people will need a mason to build homes in Kansas!"* I couldn't believe my ears. Here were my parents, nearly 50 years of age, willing to go to Kansas. My father was right, as a skilled mason, he would surely be picked for the journey. My mother smiled at him, *"You know I was really going to miss all of them."*

So it was decided. One month later, we would be ready and waiting to board the train, all four of us, to head for Kansas. My mother asked me what she should do with the letter. I said, *"Tear it up. I'm not taking any chances of not being on the next train. If Ephram wants to be with me and the children, then he can come, too. Nobody needs to know we're not married, and if all goes well, we soon will be."*

On August 29, 1854, the train left the depot in Boston. Charles H. Branscomb was the conductor. Among the passengers was a lawyer, Samuel Pomeroy, who served as the financial agent for the trip. [Pomeroy would later become the first Senator from the State of Kansas.] Charles Robinson had returned from the first trip and was intending to stay after bringing the rest of the colony to Kansas. [Robinson would become the first governor of the state of Kansas]. My parents, Daniel Sayer (age 50)and Elizabeth Jones Sayer (age 50); myself, Mary Ann Dennitt (age 30); my sons, James C. Dennitt and Squire Dennitt, and my ex-husband, Ephram H. Dennitt (age 30) were all on board. [Note: The 1855 Census has Ephram listed as <u>B</u>ennitt.] After changing to a steamboat in St. Louis, we arrived in Kansas City on September 6, 1854.

After we arrived in Kansas City, we went to the Quaker Mission twelve miles from the port. The Shawnee and Delaware Indians were superior guides. They intermarried and lived primarily around Fort Leavenworth and the Kansas City region. The Quakers formed a good relationship with them. From the Mission, we joined the rest of the New England colony at a settlement along the Wakarusa River. A Shawnee Chief, George Blue-jacket, welcomed the new settlers into his home along the Wakarusa where it joined the Kansas River [approximately 10 miles southeast of present day Lawrence]. Chief Blue-Jacket said *"Wakarusa"* meant, *"River of Big Weeds."* We lived in tents and drank water from that weedy river. Many of us got sick with the ague, presenting malaria-type symptoms, which included the shakes. Dr. John Doy, a physician from Rochester, New York, was kept very busy in those early days.

My father was given a task immediately. Several men with masonry and construction skills, were asked to build a hotel for suitable housing, until individual cabins could be built in *"new Boston."* The need for shelter was great, particularly not knowing when the first winter storm may come. The village, known as Lawrence, consisted of a few log cabins and a pole shed. The Astor House, poles that formed an A-frame with a thatch roof, served as lodging for travelers passing through. Cabins were built from cottonwood trees, which were the primary source of wood; however, as the wood dried, it tended to warp and split.

The [Douglas County] sheriff, Samuel Jones, who previously held the position of Postmaster at Westport, Missouri, was the pro-slavery watch dog. He concocted warrants for horse thieving or cattle rustling, just to way-lay progress building a hotel or individual cabins. We could not expect any protection from the military under the territorial law of *"popular sovereignty,"* besides there was a cholera epidemic at Fort Riley and all the soldiers at that fort were under quarantine.

The river was a breeding place for mosquito larvae and snakes. Gnats were thick by day, locusts by night. The cooking that I did for others was done outside, in the sun. Working over an open fire, I constantly inhaled smoke, my hands were chapped, and my skin peeled, like a snake sheds its skin. First frost brought the only relief from insect menaces whose bites became infected and covered my body.

We elected our own governing body to bring a sense of order to our colony. Dr. Charles Robinson was voted to continue as the leader. He cautioned us to not break any territorial laws, anything that would give authorities due cause, as *"Christ had instructed his own to render unto Caesar, that which is Caesar's, then so shall ye do likewise."* Confident in the political process bringing a just end, Dr. Robinson spoke on the side of peaceful constraint. He eagerly awaited the Spring elections. Second in command, Colonel James Lane, did not share Robinson's views. He was more inclined to believe that the only recourse was bloodshed.

On March 30, 1855, over a thousand Missourians overtook the town of Lawrence. Many Bushwhackers bearing pistols and knives threatened the lives of poll workers who attempted to prevent them from voting in the election since they were not residents of the territory. Dr. Robinson viewed the whole election debacle as a tactical error on the part of the Border Ruffians, who he felt did more harm than good by so openly and fraudulently controlling the election. Such actions could only create sympathy for free-soilers who were attempting to settle the territory by more diplomatic means. Dr. Robinson reassured his followers that patience would bring about the desired end result. Not everyone was willing to give the time or take the risk, and over one-third of the members of the colony returned East.

The tension within the town of Lawrence continued to mount. Nevertheless, more immigrants from the newly organized "New England Emigrant Aid Society" headed west. By late Fall, 1855, Lawrence had grown to around 200 people. Shalor Eldridge footed the bill for the new *"Free State Hotel's"* completion. The Eldridge family lived within. It stood tall and proud among shanties and chicken coops.

A claim dispute erupted in November, 1855, resulting in a slaver killing one of the free-soilers. Soon after, a band of free-soilers burnt down the cabins of some pro-slavery families in retaliation. Sheriff Jones and his posse captured who they thought was the ring leader of the group of arsonists. The free-soilers rallied and set out to rescue one of their own. After a confrontation that nearly resulted in gun fire, the prisoner was released to the vigilantes. Knowing that Sheriff Jones would not, could not, allow that to be the end of it, runners were dispatched to Topeka to rally support for what the colonists believed was an impending invasion.

Colonel Lane stepped up to take command of the voluntary militia. Even women, including myself, commenced to prepare for battle by learning how to shoot a weapon. Every available male, including Ephram and my two sons, James (15) and Squire (14) were actively engaged in training. My parents were conflicted by our involvement in the militia. Bearing arms was contrary to our religious beliefs, yet they knew without a way to protect ourselves, we were nothing more than sitting ducks. Lane had made arrangements with a Reverend Beecher from Connecticut for Sharps rifles to be delivered to Kansas under the pretense of them being Bibles. These rifles were fast-firing and accurate at long-range. Dr. Robinson hastened to amend his instructions. Again, requesting that violence be only a last resort, he reinforced his philosophy that the militia was one of *"defense,"* not *"offense."*

Meanwhile, Missourians bivouacked along the Wakarusa and prepared for war. Lawrence was surrounded. The territorial militia, stationed at Lecompton, closed in from the west; the Border Ruffians along the Wakarusa, from the east.

Reinforcements also poured in for the free-soilers. Members of the Shawnee and Delaware tribes offered their support. I thought this truly ironic, given that the Indians had been given this territory as part of a government treaty before the passage of the Kansas-Nebraska Bill of 1854. Now, tribes that were not even native to Kansas, who had been transplanted from the East, were willing to step in and help us, the very people who were displacing them.

Abolitionists from other parts of the Kansas territory, to the south and to the west, responded to the cry for help. John Brown and his four sons from Osawatomie pulled into Lawrence on December 7, 1855 in a wagon filled with navy revolvers, ammunition, and pole-bayonets. After meeting with Colonel Lane, the Browns joined forces with the volunteer militia, and John Brown was named Captain of the *"Liberty Guards."*

Territorial Governor Wilson Shannon arrived from Shawnee Mission and played the intermediary between the factions. With the help of mother nature, the Wakarusa War [as it was later labeled] came to closure.

The following day, December 8, 1855, brought a ferocious winter storm. Ice and sleet preceded snow, as temperatures ranged 20 to 30 degrees below zero. Every piece of food had to be thawed at the fire in order to eat it. Walking in the snow to cut firewood, numbed the feet and resulted in bad cases of frostbite. The fire, itself, posed a hazard. Gusting winds caused flames to dance erratically. Some people saw their small shelters go up in smoke.

In March, 1856, Dr. Charles Robinson was placed on the ballot as a free-state candidate for Governor of the State of Kansas. Free state voters came out in great numbers, winning the popular vote, and hoping to force being acknowledged as having authority in Kansas. The election results were deemed bogus since Kansas was not recognized by the United States yet as a state, but a territory.

Come April, 1856, Sheriff Jones was back in full form antagonizing an unforgiving community. Sam Wood, who had helped rescue Jones' prisoner the winter before, returned to Lawrence, setting off a series of events with no turning back. Sheriff Jones attempted to arrest Wood. When Wood refused to recognize his authority and walk away, a mob gathered. Jones, being out-numbered rode to Lecompton to request re-enforcement's. When Sheriff Jones returned with U.S. dragoons, six men were arrested. The free-soilers waited for their opportunity to take revenge on Sheriff Jones under cover of darkness. That night shots were fired. No one knew from where or from whom, and Sheriff Jones was paralyzed for life. Rumors of the Sheriff being *"assassinated"* incited the slavers into a frenzy.

Dr. Robinson, fearing the consequences of the actions of members of the community, fled. Lane, who had then become General of the militia, also left, but promised to return with more recruits. John Brown, his sons, and other members of his guard were at Osawatomie. The colony at Lawrence was never more vulnerable. Samuel Pomeroy attempted to take charge of the frightened group. Word was received that Dr. Robinson was captured on a steamboat in Lexington, Missouri. He was imprisoned at Fort Leavenworth. Nervously the free-soilers waited for the slavers to make the next move.

On May 19, 1856, Bushwhackers ended the lives of two pickets, or *"stubs"* as we called them, keeping watch near Blanton's Bridge on the Wakarusa. Ephram Dennitt was one of them. I couldn't believe my eyes when they rode into town leading Ephram's horse with his body draped over the saddle. My sorrow was only overcome by my resolve that Ephram did not die in vain. With great calmness, and inward hysteria, I begged my mother and father to take James and Squire from this God forsaken town NOW! There would be others who would take flight come next daybreak, and I felt their chances of surviving were better or equal on the prairie to waiting it out in Lawrence. At first, they wanted to argue that they would not leave unless I went, but knowing my stubbornness, responded to the urgency of saving their only grandsons, and removing them from the scene of their father's tragic death.

At dawn on May 21, 1856, the folks at Lawrence awakened to the sight of hundreds of Border Ruffians outlining the perimeter of Mount Oread. Sheriff Jones met with Samuel Pomeroy and ordered that he have the citizens abandon their arms. The free-soilers were told, *"Even the women, if they carry rifles, will be blown to hell with a chunk of lead."* Pomeroy protested, saying that the arms were private property.

Then Sheriff Jones advised Shalor Eldridge to vacate the Free State Hotel. If he wished to save any of his belongings, he had best move them forthwith. The *Herald of Freedom* press was destroyed with axe and sledgehammers. A cannon was wheeled into town and fired repeatedly at the hotel. Ammo was exploded in the basement of the hotel, and still she stood. Finally, through fire, the Free State fortress was in shambles. Dr. Robinson's home was burnt to the ground, as well. The ascending Border Ruffians were a petrifying sight, sending free-soilers screaming into the streets, desperately seeking shelter from Armageddon.

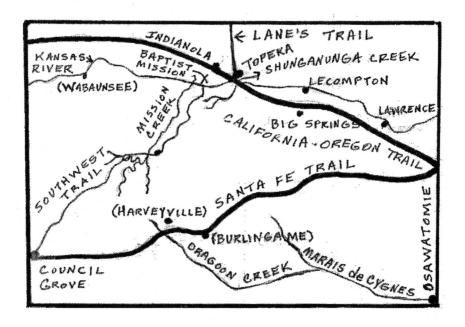

After Lawrence was sacked, my father, Daniel Sayer, knew there would be little time to get me out of Lawrence, if I had survived. Our cabin was still standing. I had given shelter to others who were less fortunate. In tears, I clung to my father who bravely returned to take me with him. He said that their group of wagons had headed due west to Big Springs, staying south of Lecompton, in hopes of making it to Topeka. Fortunately, a Shawnee Indian scout spied the group and shepherded them to a bend on a creek known as the Shunganunga. From there they could follow the creek north to Topeka. The caravan chose to remain in the remote location, sheltered by the natural terrain along the creek's edge until Daniel Sayer returned. I escaped Lawrence with the clothes on my back, my Sharps rifle, and a saddle bag of ammo.

We decided that it would be best to stay where we were along the Shunga-nunga. My father and I had been able to return without being followed. All of us would take turns keeping watch several yards from camp where we could get a fairly good view of anyone approaching. Every time we built a fire we ran the risk of being found, but we knew if we did not boil the creek water, we would all become sick with the ague and unable to protect ourselves. Besides, the wildlife along the creek would sustain us, and fire was needed to cook rabbits and turkey. The men fell some cottonwood trees so we had sufficient firewood. We lived out of the wagons encircled there.

During the times that I kept watch, I reflected on the events that had led to our being there. I was not sorry that I had come to Kansas. Maybe I felt like working for the greater good would somehow redeem me for the mistakes I had made. I had known it wasn't going to be easy, but never in my wildest dreams did I anticipate the violence! The good that had come was that my sons had gotten to know the father that I knew Ephram could be, not the father of their birth. Ephram had shown strength and courage. He had become a solid man; one that his sons had learned to respect. We would have surely remarried had we not been delivered into a hot bed of strife. At the time, getting married again was the last thing on either of our minds. Only survival mattered. If I were sorry for anything, it was for getting my mother and father involved in all of this. If we survived the conflict at hand, I would encourage them to go far away from this place.

This place, Kansas, however, grows on you. Never had I lived any place that had such varied seasons. For all its pestilence, which no one in their right mind could abide, the seasons brought forth magnificent beauty. Even the snowstorm of a wicked winter created a security blanket when militia movement was checked, and all was quiet about you, glistening, being cleansed for a new begin-ning. Despite prairie fire, wind, or ice, the resilient land would come to life in the spring. In a way, it was symbolic of the people I had come to know. Those of us who had stayed in Kansas, knew that we, too, would rise again, stronger and more determined than before. For the first time in weeks, I was able to rest and enjoy the sounds of summer about me, the Kansas wildflowers, and gentle breezes.

I believe nearly a month had passed, when a group of men were spotted very late one night. Their silhouettes were barely noticeable in the moonlight. They must have seen the smoke from our camp fire. Our lookout slithered back to camp on his belly. The flames from the fire were immediately doused with water. Each of us grabbed a weapon and scooted under our wagons. If this was the end, then we would take a few down with us. I could barely hear low whispering as the men cautiously approached. When they were within shot, my father yelled out, "Halt! Or we'll shoot!" There was a pause, then a reply, "Are you opposed to the Northern or free state party?"

I recognized the voice, "Captain Brown?" I inquired.

"As I live and breathe," was the reply. "We mean you no harm."

My father responded, "Approach slowly and show yourself. We will recognize John Brown." The men came out into the open, with guns still drawn.

"It is Captain Brown," I said to my father, as I recognized him from when he and his sons had brought weapons to Lawrence and joined up with the volunteer militia. We threw out our guns from under the wagons, "We are free-soilers, Captain Brown."

John Brown and his followers camped with us that evening. He reported that free-soilers who had fled to Kansas City to board steamboats back North, were being hunted down by the Bushwhackers. Some had even been pulled from hotel beds and murdered. All steamboat traffic on the Missouri was being boarded at Lexington and then also at Westport in search of contraband, and persons from the North were being jailed (if they were lucky) until they could be shipped back. Leaders of the colony in Lawrence, including Dr. Robinson who was first held in Leavenworth, were herded to Lecompton where they were imprisoned.

"They have even put my son, John Brown Jr. behind bars! General Lane will not rest until he has brought reinforcements from the North."

Brown told us of a plan they had for marking a trail that would bring emigrants into Kansas from the north, rather than the east.

"Even before the massacre at Lawrence, we knew we would have to devise another way to bring in firearms after Beecher's Bibles were discovered. Now, we shall escort an army from the North into Kansas and we will kill our oppressors, as David killed Goliath!"

Before daybreak, Brown and his followers had headed north along the Shunganunga to Topeka where the free-state party intended to regroup and convene its legislature. He encouraged us to do likewise. Bivouacked to the east of Topeka were Governor Shannon's militia who had been directed to "scatter the outlaws in Topeka." As it turned out, the few hundred free-staters that materialized, were not enough to resist the orders of Colonel Sumner for the free-state legislature to disband (July 4, 1856). The down-trodden free-soilers lost all hope. John Brown knew that he must get in contact with General Lane immediately!

Members of our party dispersed. Most of us stayed in Topeka. Without any capital to relocate, we decided to dig into the banks of the Shunganunga where we would at least have shelter for the winter. We found an area that already formed a cave-like opening and yet was far enough beneath the bank to withstand being shallowed out even more. In the hot July sun, we worked diligently to carve a shelter from the earth. My father learned that limestone was being quarried on the John Ritchie farm, a short distance from where we staked our claim. He called on John Ritchie to see if, in exchange for his masonry skills, we might have some of the rubble to help shore up the cave. Ritchie knew that Daniel Sayer would be an asset to his ambitions of building a town, and agreed readily. *"Besides, one never knows when having a cave near by will come in handy,"* quipped John Ritchie.

Rumors spread throughout Topeka that John Brown and a group of vigilantes took it upon themselves to get revenge for the sacking of Lawrence. On May 24, 1856, in the valley along Pottawatomie Creek which was near Brown's home of Osawatomie, John Brown released his outrage on innocent pioneers. A saber was taken to the dog at the farm of James and Mahala Doyle. Mr. Doyle and two of his sons were walked outside where John Brown shot James Doyle in the head, and Brown's sons hacked the two Doyle boys to death. Allen Wilkinson, owner of the next cabin they happened upon, was slain, also by sword. Finally, William Sherman, who was sleeping at the James Harris cabin, was escorted to Pottawatomie Creek where he, too, was murdered.

I did not believe these lies to be true! I felt certain that slavers had embellished the facts, and refused to believe that Captain Brown would be so cold-blooded unless he knew these men to be involved in the murdering and raiding of Lawrence! Captain Brown had not once mentioned while in our camp that he had taken any actions in retaliation for what happened at Lawrence, even after I had told him about Ephram being killed while serving as a picket.

Supplies ran low for free-soilers who had made the exodus from their promised land. The Border Ruffians had been successful in cutting off most of the shipments into Topeka and Lawrence, where trade was essential to their survival.

General Lane remained true to his word, he had recruited a wagon train of northern settlers to come to Topeka. New weapons and men were a shot in the arm to the weary free-soilers. Many of the Topeka men, in a quandary as to how to handle the shortage of food and supplies, turned to General Lane, for guidance. Gone were the days of Robinson's passive resistance. General Lane led several raids on neighboring communities, including the pro-slavery communities of Indianola and Tecumseh. Free-staters felt empowered once more!

Nearly 50 raiders were arrested for their part in the raids. John Ritchie was one of them. Mary Jane Ritchie, who had only recently given birth, despaired over her husband being arrested and imprisoned at Lecompton. Our family befriended Mary Jane and her children. Around the first of December we heard that thirty of the prisoners had escaped on November 21, 1856, by *"pegging a hole in the wall and crawling out like rats."* Weeks passed and Mary Jane did not know if her husband was dead or alive. Finally a letter was received from Indiana. John had made it safely out of Kansas and was staying at his father's home, until it would be safe to return to Kansas.

Occasionally, I would call on Mary Jane Ritchie and we would talk. Sometimes my mother, Elizabeth Sayer, would look after the baby so that Mary Jane could get out of the house for a while. I confided in her about my *"husband"* being killed and what my life had been like in Lawrence. I also told her about the Shawnee Indian scout who helped my parents, sons, and others find safety after Lawrence was sacked, and about the surprise visit from John Brown in our camp that night. We commiserated about how quickly some would turn their backs on Captain Brown. I insisted that she let me teach her how to shoot a Sharps rifle, since her husband owned one. I took Mary Jane to the Shunganunga where she learned how to aim and fire. The winter passed.

In March, 1857, something more deadly than Border Ruffians was in the wind: SMALL POX. We had heard of small pox wiping out entire Indian villages, so when the first case arrived in Topeka, people quarantined themselves into their homes. We had spent a lot of time that winter discussing where we might go and what we might do. I knew I wanted my parents to find a nice piece of land where they could build a home—some place away from the politics of the territory. My father had heard about a southwest trail leading to Council Grove. There was a lot of bottom land as it followed Mission Creek where crops should grow in the fertile soil, and there was also a lot of native limestone. James and Squire could farm the land if we could procure some implements. With the arrival of disease, the plan went into action with more urgency.

John Ritchie returned from Indiana. There was a joyous reunion in the Ritchie household. My father told Mr. Ritchie that he would like to continue to work for him as a stone mason. The money he earned in wages could be used to purchase farm implements so that his grandsons could work a claim. He promised to return to Topeka as soon as we had staked a claim southwest of Topeka and built temporary lodging. John Ritchie concurred that he thought he would continue to need Daniel Sayer for goals he had to build commercial buildings to build up the town of Topeka. And did 1857 ever bring building opportunities in Topeka! People from the north moved down Lane's trail in droves. Topeka grew to over 450 people that spring. Daniel Sayer became one of several masons needed to build whole blocks of commercial buildings, including hotels to house new residents while they built their homes. The limestone was mined from the Shunganunga and lime mortar burnt in a lag heap along its banks. Three sides of the buildings were built from the native limestone, but the front walls were faced with brick and other embellishments, such as columns and arches. At last my father was again using the skills God had given him.

With experience in building a cabin and building a dug-out, we decided that both had their advantages. A cabin allowed for circulation, visibility, and space. A dug-out provided insulation and safety. My sons were instructed to dig a hole in the ground several yards from the creek's edge. The ground along the creek bank wasn't as compact as field land. Tree roots can be both a help and a hindrance. Roots keep the soil loose, but they also act like a reinforcement in holding soil together. The disadvantage is that they are an obstacle to digging. A hatchet took care of the roots handily. The ground temperature closer to water was cooler.

The hole in the ground was squared up to measure six feet across by ten feet in length. We made the width narrower so that it was easier to find and fell trees that were about eight feet tall, cut in half with a saw and laid side by side across the six foot width. On the east end, away from Mission Creek, we dug out in an incline so we could access the eight foot depth. The split wood on top was camouflaged with prairie grasses tied to the wood. Our door was also made of split wood that was put in place from the inside.

My father met other men, including the Sage brothers and the Haskells, who had taught themselves how to cut the limestone into blocks, and had a system already in place. They were laying the foundations of two houses, less than half a mile from our dug-out. The men were glad to know Daniel Sayer and to be able to inquire about technique, mortar, weight-bearing load, and so forth. My father asked Squire and James if they would help the others on their homes. This way they would learn how to cut the blocks and we could line the interior of the dug-out with limestone. Meanwhile, Daniel Sayer could return to Topeka to work at the Ritchie quarry.

My mother and I became acquainted with the Sage women, Mary Ann, Elizabeth, Ann, and Josephine. We were by far out numbered by the men in the area. We were within easy walking distance of one another and so when one of us had a chore to do, we'd all help one another. The time would pass more quickly and our friendship grew. Mother and I were a steady source of information about the politics of the state, since my father would come home periodically and bring us up to date about the goings on in Topeka. For instance, the free state legislature reconvened in Constitution Hall [Farnsworth building in Topeka] after being forbidden to do so the year before. Attempts to prevent its existence tended to only fuel the flame. In fact, Topeka was setting its sights on replacing Lecompton as the capital of a FREE state. If the women had a preference for being passive about the fight at hand, they soon learned not to express that to me. I was willing to pledge whatever support I could, if it would result in Kansas becoming a free state.

In early November, 1857, several of the local men, including my sons, went to a rally called by Captain Brown's followers. I knew it was only a matter of time before James and Squire would feel they had come into their own manhood and were ready to join the cause. I was very proud of them and encouraged them to go with the rest as they rode to a farm outside of Lawrence. Several days later when they returned they told me that they would have gone with John Brown had he intended to remain in Kansas but the reason for the meeting was to recruit for a show-down in Virginia. James and Squire had promised their grandfather to finish working on our dug out. The roof would need to be replaced before the first snow. I knew this would not be their last opportunity to take a more active role.

My father showed not only James and Squire, but also the other men, how to cut wedge-shaped stones to make archways that would support weight from above. The weight actually created pressure against the wedges making them tighter. Daniel Sayer could cut stones with the precision of puzzle pieces. Our dug-out became their training ground as they perfected putting an arched ceiling that spanned a six foot width. Mark Sage became really skilled at archway masonry. Years later he would design bridges and barns, using this arch as his signature trademark. After the mortar was dry, approximately six inches of dirt was compacted over the top. A pipe was inserted for circulation during the winter when the door would need to be placed over the opening. After the first snow, we all laughed heartily when the Sages literally had to *"dig us out."* The snow drifted into the incline opening and filled the area next to the door. We exited, and teased right back that at least our shoes were dry!

By Spring, 1858, my father had purchased a milk cow, four additional oxen and 24" breaking plow for us to put in our first crops along Mission Creek. Squire and James learned a great deal about farming from the Sages. I think they thought of Alfred and John as big brothers. My father continued to work in Topeka. Most of the time he would stay in the dug-out along the Shunganunga because it took a full day to ride to Mission Creek from Topeka. He would come home between jobs and then stay for a few days at a time before returning to start work on another Ritchie project. After the crops were in the field, we were able to start building the cabin above the dug-out to finish our home.

My father met William T. Berryman in Topeka. He, and his wife, Hannah, had come from Illinois. After getting their wagon across by Pappan's ferry, W. T. knew his oxen could not make it any further. They had become ill and were not doing well on the last leg of the journey. Berryman went to the town livery where he found an old Indian man working. He told W.T. that with some doctoring, the oxen should get better. In order to pay for the care of his oxen, Berryman took a job working for Cyrus K. Holliday splitting logs. He got paid 60 cents for 100 rails. When my father found out that Hannah was staying in the wagon with their two children, and W.T. boarding with the oxen, he offered them shelter in the dug-out on the Shunganunga.

In a short time, the Berryman's oxen were ready to move on. After visiting with Daniel Sayer, they, too, decided to turn their wagon southwest to the Mission Creek area. My father told W. T. that he would pay him as a log splitter after he arrived, if he would help his grandsons finish the cabin.

The Berryman's were impressed with the natural shelter provided by a large cliff southwest of where the Sayer's claim was located. The area was also along the creek, and W. T. Berryman thought it would be a natural location to create a dug-out similar to the one where Daniel Sayer had let them stay on the Shunganunga. There was just one problem, the land was already claimed by James Bassett. So Berryman's found a wooded lot not far from John Sage's cabin.

James Bassett had not built on the cliff land; he was gone much of the time freighting grain to and from Denver and Taos with Mark Sage. In fact, he'd even told John he might stay out in Denver to do some prospecting as it was rumored that some miners had struck gold. When John told him that his new neighbors had their eye on living by the cliffs, James told John to tell them he'd switch lots with them. The only thing he cared about was having a wooded area as a source for fuel whenever he did build.

After searching the cliff dwelling well, Berryman found a cave that was used by Indians. As far as any of us knew, there had not been any Indians living there since 1854. They found many artifacts to substantiate the existence of an entire village, but likely from many, many years before. W. T. liked to take his little two year old, Elizabeth, to the top of the cliff where he would cup his hands and yell,

"Hello." Libby's eyes would light up in amazement as the echo back would yell, "Hello. Hello." [Echo Cliff has yielded artifacts that date back to the time of the Woodland Indians during the Grasshopper Falls phase, 1000 A.D.]

By the time the Sayer's cabin was completed, Berryman found out that James had, in fact, stayed in Denver, so he approached Mark about taking James' place freighting, until James Bassett returned and was ready to work again with Mark, of course. So W. T. earned money for his family doing that line of work for the first year and a half after he came to Mission Creek.

Friend Henry Harvey was a Quaker missionary to the Osage Indians who lived on Dragoon Creek with his wife, Ann, and two sons, Samuel and Saul. I was always fascinated by their stories of the Indians that lived in this area when they first came in 1840. They had been guests at many lodges where they learned the language of the tribe and used sign and drawings to communicate about the Quaker beliefs. I was surprised to learn that the Indians had a creation story similar to the Genesis of our own beliefs. We were very much in alignment with our feelings about freedom and stewardship. My family made a point of worshipping with the Harvey's, if not weekly, then at least a couple of times each month. We would either drive to their cabin several miles south or they would join us in our home on Mission Creek, for a Sunday afternoon Bible study and prayer.

The Loomis family also came to Mission Creek in 1858, after having spent the winter at the Topeka House. The Loomis' had more money to start life on the prairie than most of us. Harvey came from Winsor, Connecticut where his family had started the Loomis Institute, a preparatory school for boys. I liked his wife, Sara Ann, very much because she was also a native of Pennsylvania. Sara was the only person I ever told about being married to a lawyer in Erie. Harvey Loomis made two trips back and forth to Topeka with his oxen right after staking his claim. He brought back wagon loads of split logs to build their cabin. Realizing that there may be an opportunity to sell building materials to others, he started his own business.

The Sage's welcomed Samuel Sage Jr., Alfred, John and Mark's younger brother in 1858. He was a handsome young man. We didn't really get to know him very well because he joined the volunteer militia under General Lane right after he arrived.

The crops grew well for our first year as farmers! The closest grist mill was in Auburn (some people still referred to it as Brownville). We'd give the miller a sack of flour for his services. Mother and I would make sweet cream and butter from Bessie. My mother, Elizabeth Sayer, could bake the most wonderful bread! She and I had put in a garden, in addition to the boys planting field crops. We anxiously waited for the vines to mature and fruits to ripen. Maybe it was true after all, what they had told us back in New England, about Kansas being the world's garden.

Sometime during the summer months (1858), my father told us that Topeka was buzzing with news that five free soilers had been killed along the Marais des Cygnes. Captain Brown was back in Kansas and had joined forces with James Montgomery, the leader of the Jayhawks, who were set on returning *"an eye for an eye."* The Jayhawks reputation was parallel to the Bushwhackers as they pillaged farms and stole cattle of Southern settlers. In February they had raided Fort Scott, a pro-slave stronghold. Many free soil activists cheered their efforts, but many did not. Dr. Robinson was released from the Lecompton jail after Governor Geary took office. He maintained a following of those trying to bring a peaceful disposition to the conflict between the free soilers and pro-slavery factions. While I admired his convictions, we had seen for ourselves that there would be no diplomatic resolution.

One evening when it was near sundown, Alfred Sage dropped by for a visit. It was odd for him to come without Mary Ann, but he came alone, hat in hand. Alfred joined mother and me, James and Squire, at the table. He told us that Samuel had knowledge of Captain Brown being ill and of his whereabouts. He said that after what happened along the Marais des Cygnes, John Brown was ready to steal slaves from the Bushwhackers. It was as if they were taunting him, daring him to continue on with his crusade, which of course, has made him all the more determined, but the slaves would need a place to go. Alfred said he had promised Captain Brown that if he ever freed any of the slaves, he could count on him for assistance in keeping them safe while he orchestrated their travel to Canada. He said he feared that the time had come, and questioned whether we would be receptive to hiding any slaves that came to Mission Creek. He said there was the possibility that we would not be called upon; then again, we had the ideal place for hiding someone.

When we built our cabin, we did not build it directly above the dug-out. Instead, the west side of it was placed over the incline into the underground room. We laid a floor in the cabin of smooth flat limestone rocks that we pulled up from the creek bed by rope tied to our ox. We built a wood platform for a bed over the opening that could be pulled out from the wall when access was needed. When the bed was in place against the west wall, you couldn't tell but what the stone flooring was under the bed. Indeed, why would you think anything else? Neither of us were hesitant to give Alfred an answer. We knew Daniel Sayer would concur, as well. My family were Quakers. We did not believe in any kind of human bondage. If Captain Brown needed us to provide food and lodging for runaway slaves, we would do so.

It was the day before Christmas, and we thought, perhaps, we had not been needed to assist Alfred. I did not discuss the visit with his wife, Mary Ann, as I was not at all certain whether Mary Ann even knew that Alfred was involved. Then we noticed that Alfred was gone. Mary Ann acted as if there was nothing unusual about Alfred being gone so close to Christmas, but I had my suspicions. The night came, a knock at the door, a hoarse whisper, *"Mary Ann, Mary Ann, it's Alfred Sage."*

I lit the candle beside the bed and went to the door. Alfred was standing there—alone. *"What is it?"* I asked.

"I have a Negro with me. She's with child. She's pretty worn out. Can you and your mother look after her?"

I nodded, yes. Alfred then motioned for her to come out from the trees along the creek. She stepped inside and Alfred was gone into the night. He went home to celebrate Christmas with his family.

Alfred Sage left again after Christmas, was gone off and on for the next month, but in February announced to family and friends that John Brown had successfully gotten eleven slaves to Nebraska where they would head for Canada and freedom. Captain Brown said he would not return as it was time to draw attention to another part of the country. We could only speculate that he was headed to Virginia where the year before he had tried to get others to accompany him.

The Spring weather for 1859, began much the same as it had the year before. Crops did well, but because of the glut from the year before, we could only get 15 cents per bushel for the corn, and only then after taking it to Leavenworth. The Topeka market was not able to buy more.

A large fire sent the *Kansas State Record* in Topeka up in blazes that summer. Topeka had no emergency fire assistance and the water in the Kansas River was at a record low. The newspaper had been operated by one of the Ross brothers. The Ross's had pre-empted land a few miles from us.

By Fall, however, what corn hadn't been harvested had burnt in the fields. The prairie grasses died early. It was going to be a hard winter on our livestock. Little did we know at the time that we were headed for one of the worst droughts in the history of the territory.

W. T. Berryman began working for Harvey Loomis as a log splitter. His stint working with Mark Sage had lasted longer than he had expected since James Bassett did strike gold and worked a claim in the Pike's Peak region. But after the claim busted, James returned and purchased land adjacent to the wooded lot Berryman had traded him, which was next to John and Elizabeth Sage's land.

My father came back to Mission Creek to spend the rest of the winter. Activity at the quarry was slow. Those who had initiated construction, were now guarding their livelihood in case they would need the reserve, concerned about the changing climate. John Ritchie gave my father the news about Captain Brown being defeated—and disappointed—at Harper's Ferry. When the stage was set, most of the Negroes he thought would show to help him in the raid, didn't show. Instead, the Captain was hanged. When you hear news like that, you wonder if all of it had been for naught. I felt downtrodden; an idealist with a dream. Had it all been folly?

The winter was cold and dry. I had an ash hopper that I put wood ash in from the stove. When it rained, lye was made from the soot. I hauled buckets of water from the creek and poured into the hopper. I boiled this liquid with grease and made soap, which was also something I could sell in Topeka. There was very little snow, so that by the following spring, it was impossible to plow the fields! Beef was in short supply, so we salted and smoked some for reserve. The Indians became very forward in their desire to have food from our homes. I learned to tell them *"pawkey chee,"* which meant *"please leave."* I was not afraid of them like some of the women in our village, and just like with animals, I think they sensed that I couldn't be intimidated.

John Ritchie continued to assist slaves by hiding them in a series of locations throughout Topeka as they followed the path of that first group led by John Brown. My father said there were some that stayed with him in the cave on the Shunganunga. On April 20, 1860, a Deputy U.S. Marshal went to John Ritchie's home to arrest him. Ritchie, who was outside at the time, walked inside his house and picked up a pistol. The Marshal followed him to make his arrest. Ritchie turned around and shot the Marshal, the ball piercing him in the neck. Ritchie surrendered himself to the local Justice of the Peace, but sympathies of the town folks brought an indictment of justifiable homicide.

In early summer, Simon and Ann Main's children became deathly ill with high fever which left them limp as dish rags. I had gotten to know Ann, who was Alfred Sage's sister. Mother and I both helped her nurse the little ones during this time, since the other women had young ones at home that they couldn't leave. Elizabeth Sage's little girl came down with the same thing, probably before Elizabeth knew it was contagious. First a dry cough, then air passages start to shut down on them. We began boiling everything that the young ones came in contact with. Sadly, the Main daughters both died, as did the Sage girl. Ann's sons recuperated; but there was a horrible dark cloud hanging over the valley. The whole Sage family was so broken up, that I asked my boys if they would build the tiny wooden coffins. Father St. John, whose family had only recently moved across the road and east of the Haskell place, handled the service.

The Government sent disaster relief money, food, supplies to the territory in the fall, after having all crops fail. We were able to pick up what we needed from John and Alfred Sage after they started a store in a log cabin. They would make trips to Leavenworth to get the subsidy from Samuel Pomeroy who acted as the government's distribution agent.

Abraham Lincoln was elected to become the next President in November, 1860, and immediately the South was up in arms. As states made their plans for secession, my own sons, James and Squire were telling Momma and Granny that they were joining the Kansas Cavalry! Winter drug on and then on January 21,

1861, Kansas was voted a free state! After six long years of fighting this battle, we claimed victory!!! Dr. Charles Robinson was officially recognized by Congress as the first state governor (1861–1863). James Lane and Samuel Pomeroy were elected our new state senators.

Well, having Kansas, admitted to the Union as a free state was the spark that lit the cannon. By April, President Lincoln could tell that our country was headed for a Civil War. My sons, James and Squire Dennitt, along with James Bassett, Samuel Sage, Edmund Ross, George Ross, William Ross, and John St. John all rode to Topeka to join the Cavalry. Several local men also went to join the volunteer militia, and were willing to fight, in the event of aggression upon Kansas. Their commitment was solely for protection of Kansas citizens WITHIN the boundaries of Kansas. Their original term was set for 90 days in which they felt confident that the Union would by then have won the war.

James, Squire, James Bassett, Samuel Sage, and William Ross were all assigned to 2nd Kansas Cavalry. Edmund Ross, George Ross and John St. John were assigned to the 11th. Alfred Sage, John Sage, William Berryman, Harvey Loomis, Albert, Jacob and Thomas Haskell, Simon Main, Sylvester and Walter Ross all joined the 2nd regiment of the Kansas State Militia (K.S.M.). Alfred Sage was made a Sergeant because of his previous experience with the militia.

April also brought rain—lots of it! My father came home to take over farming. John Ritchie had gone to fight for his country. Mark Sage had completed the construction of his own stone home during the drought and was working on a stagecoach station for John Copp about five miles west. Mark and my father had gotten to be great friends, so together they worked on arched bridges that forged streams in the area which greatly enhanced transportation.

The stagecoach would bring mail from Leavenworth and drop it off at the Sage store for those of us who lived near by. I'd watch for the stage which would pass right on the corner of our place. Alfred Sage said the concord coach kind of reminded him of an English tax car. The wheels were five to six feet apart with white oak supporting stout osnaburg. The benches inside had leather cushions. The mail was stashed under the seats so I'd see the passengers politely get out and let the driver pull out the pouches. I knew if the stage had stopped on its way to Copp's Station, someone in Mission Creek had gotten lucky.

Waiting for that first letter when you're a mother whose two sons have gone to war can seem like an eternity. I had always been very protective of my boys, yet I wanted them to become men that others respected, too. Alfred sympathized with my loneliness and eagerness to hear from them. When at last the day arrived, I didn't receive much more than a couple of lines letting me know that they were stationed at Fort Scott. Men! We're to assume that everything's all right unless we hear something different.

Finally in the late Fall, I received another letter, a little better than the first, but not much.

Ma—

Say hello to granny and gramps. Tell them not to worry, their grandsons have found a bonded relationship with their mounts. Likely, our trustworthy horses will be more faithful than any female! Seriously, we have spent much time in drills with our mounts, teaching our horses to perceive our every order. We will likely stay at Fort Scott until the first of the year. Then it's on to Arkansas! General Curtis says we must keep Johnny Rebs from entering Missouri. Tell Granny, I'd give anything for a big slice of her bread after a diet of hard tack! Squire has been promoted to Corporal already. Love you, ma. James

When Mary Ann Sage received a letter from her brother, James Bassett, she would come over to read it to me. A week before the letter was written, the Cavalry had engaged in a skirmish at Pea Ridge. James said the Rebs had Indians fighting for them and that he had received an injury to his eye. Now I waited, worried, wondering.

The next letter came from Squire.

Ma,

We got them Rebs on the run! We've been riding the trails of northern Arkansas. Seen much activity along the Mississippi to the east. We need to break up the confederates control over the river. Feds sent a gunboat to Memphis and we were there for back-up. We took Fort Pillow so we've opened up the ol' Miss to Vicksburg. James is doing fine, but just in case he decides to say something, figure I'd better tell you first. I took some lead in my right thigh at Pea Ridge. It's all fine, Ma. I may wind up limping but you can't tell me from any other proud soldier when I'm on my mount.

I think I ought to also tell you that I've been writing to Eliza Smith and I've even gotten a couple letters in return. She's Sidney Smith's daughter, the fella that operates the ferry over by the Baptist Mission. I've never mentioned her to you before, but I'd visit with her sometimes when I'd take grain to Topeka. Every once in a while she'd be in Mission Creek to see her sister, Isabel, the school marm. The last time I saw her, she said she'd be pleased if I'd write to her. That was the day we rode to Topeka to join the Cavalry. So see, Ma, James may have fallen for his horse, but there's hope for me yet!

I'm kind of curious about something. One of the soldiers was telling about the battle at Shiloh. Guess General Grant was on the losing end of things until a General Buell rode in as back-up with fresh troops. He attacked the Rebs and General-in-

Chief Johnston was struck by a cannon-ball. I've never heard anyone else with the last name of Buell, but you, Ma. Do you suppose Lucian is fighting on the side of the Feds?

Well, we'll be covering a lot of territory over the next few months. By the time this war is over we will have criss-crossed Arkansas several times. Your loving son, Squire

Just the thought of my sweet son, being wounded, but he reassured me that he was as well as one could be after being shot. It was too close. My prayers needed to be even more fervent and persistent. Goodness, I hadn't given any thought to Lucian in such a long time. I'm sure the name of the General he mentioned had to be a coincidence because Lucian would have had to have changed his convictions to be taking such an active role. Then again, our states were not at war with one another when I had left Pennsylvania. Times like these, it would be difficult to straddle a fence, and since he was an educated man, perhaps?

The Sage store became a meeting place for those of us who had loved ones in service. The first of the year, Fannie Ross received news that the Cavalry had engaged in battle at Prairie Grove, Arkansas in December. She said as far as she knew, none of the men from Mission Creek were injured. In fact, two of the companies were ordered back to Kansas because of the guerrilla wars, but Edmund had not told her which ones. These guerrillas were deserters from the Confederate Army, a bunch of outlaws who cared little about the politics of war, but simply thirsted for the blood of free-soilers. I thought to myself in fear, my sons could be returning to the scene of where their father had died.

On August 20, 1863, a gang of guerrillas under the leadership of William Quantrell crossed the Missouri River and rode until daybreak to Lawrence, Kansas. Guards were posted around the town to prevent escape. The citizens of Lawrence were massacred without any sign of resistance on their part. Bodies were found in wells, shot to death in heaps, or burned inside their homes. I could not stand to hear the wretched details. I thought surely Lawrence was cursed. But where was the Cavalry? Hadn't Fannie Ross said they were to be stationed there? The answer came over the next several days when it was learned that the Cavalry had been moved at the request of the people of Lawrence who objected to the noise of the young men near by.

I couldn't believe my eyes when I saw a young Cavalry officer come riding down the trail, turning into the path leading to our cabin. Squire? Squire was home. He was mustered from service after reporting to Lawrence in August. He dismounted and came limping towards me as I ran to greet him. I knew that something must be wrong for my son to depart from serving his country. First, he assured us that James was all right. James was in Missouri and had been assigned to the 11th. After an hour of telling war stories to humor Granny and Gramps,

Squire removed his uniform to show a swollen limb with red streaks. He said the surgeon in his company said it looked like lead poisoning, *"but I wasn't going to let him cut off my leg, Ma. I wasn't much use to them with a bum leg so they sent me home."* I thought, if only Dr. Beach were still in Mission Creek, he'd know what to do, but Dr. Beach had enlisted in the 8th Kansas Army in May.

My father said we should take Squire in the spring wagon to Topeka. *"There is a doctor, A. J. Huntoon, who may be able to help."* Squire thought it was nonsense to transport him in a wagon, after all, he'd just spent the last several days on a horse riding to Mission Creek. I insisted. While Squire was concerned about his leg, I was concerned about his LIFE!

Dr. Huntoon did amputate Squire's leg after heavily sedating him with morphine. Squire was deeply depressed that we would allow them to take his leg, but we could not just stand by and watch him die. When Squire was able to be moved, we made the trip back home. Squire did not want Eliza Smith to know he was home, or what had happened, so we honored his wishes and kept him well hidden when crossing on the ferry. Squire fell into depression and was quite despondent throughout the winter.

In October, 1863, I was in the Sage store when a telegram was delivered reporting that Dr. Beach had died. One of Alfred Sage's duties was to personally deliver such news. He said, *"It is the least I can do to try to prepare them for the shock, and be there to lend a comforting arm."*

Mary Ann Sage was pregnant with Alfred and her's fifth child, which was due in December, 1863. No one was able to prepare Alfred for the shock of Mary Ann dying in child birth. Everyone in our community loved Mary Ann. She and Alfred were kind, gentle people. The out-pouring of love for Alfred and the children that Christmas was overwhelming.

As the stagecoach brought more and more white families to the area, there was a noticeable difference in the degree of civility that existed between the settlers and the Indians. It's hard to say who they resented more, the folks going on to Denver, Santa Fe, or California, who were disturbing their hunting grounds and killing the buffalo for sport; or the settlers who stopped to stake still another claim in the decreasing land left for them. Sporadically, some Indians would decide to exercise their resistance to the white man. In the early 1860's some Cavalry units were assigned to posts along the various trails in Kansas to escort mail stages and wagon trains. In early 1864, the 11th Kansas Cavalry was assigned to stage watch at Fort Larned after a stagecoach was abducted enroute from Council Grove.

In January, 1864, when Squire was not showing any signs of pulling himself out of his depression, my father tried to convince Squire that he should claim the land west of us, across the creek. He reminded him that several new settlers had already taken up many claims in the area after the Homestead Act of 1862 went into effect in January, 1863. Squire wanted to feel sorry for himself and protested that he could never build anything, let alone farm it. My father assured him that as soon as the winter broke, he would help Squire build his own place. He thought once he got Squire started, he might be surprised at how much he could do for himself. Squire agreed to give it a try, but if he was unable to handle it, he would relinquish it to James when he returned from service in the Cavalry.

Squire and his granddad were working on building the cabin that Spring when Squire received a surprise visitor. Eliza Smith had heard from her sister, Isabel, that Squire was home and living along Mission Creek. The poor girl was probably worried sick that Squire may have been killed, when she stopped receiving letters. I knew if her feelings were genuine, it would only be a matter of time before she came to inquire. Squire was greatly flustered, but Eliza was reassuring. Squire found that she fit perfectly under his arm and was the best looking "crutch" any man could have. It was obvious that she loved my son. Still I think Squire had doubts, worrying that she simply pitied him, so I advised him to give the relationship some time, then he would know.

Meanwhile, my own heart strings were being tugged. I didn't know myself if I was merely feeling pity, or if I was having genuine feelings for Alfred Sage. Here was a man with five children, the oldest, eight years, and the youngest a babe in arms. His sister, Ann, and his sister-in-laws were wonderful about integrating the children into their own homes so that Alfred could continue to work in the store, but they had several young ones of their own to look after so sometimes I'd request to spend some time with the kids. I'd tell Alfred that ma and I would enjoy the company. It'd been many years since we'd had any little ones around. I knew he was glad for the offer, and they were good kids.

Elizabeth Sage told me Alfred received a letter from his brother, Aaron, who was a cannoneer on a Union frigate, the end of February, 1864. Elizabeth told me that her husband, John, had written to Aaron after Mary Ann had died. She said Aaron conveyed having feelings of helplessness, and she added, *"We all do."* Aaron said the Confederates tried to retake Newbern, North Carolina, but they had successfully foiled the attempt.

Sometimes I'd try to envision what it would be like, raising small kids again and all. But, I'd scold myself. Alfred Sage couldn't possibly develop feelings for me. I was fifteen years older than him, and not likely to have ever been as pretty as his wife Mary Ann, even when I was her age. But, I sure liked Alfred. He wasn't like some men who talked down to a woman. When I'd be in the store, he'd talk to me about what was going on in our state, about events he'd heard of in the war, what we needed to do to build up a town around here. He treated me like an equal, like he really valued by opinion about things. Finally, I did say something about it to my ma. You know what she said? Love was highly over-rated. She said in our day and age we've got to take our opportunities when they come, and live our lives as if there are no tomorrow's.

In April, 1864, the Sage's were hit again with tragic news. Just a few days before a telegraph arrived at the store, Alfred had received a letter from Samuel saying that he was quarantined in Lawrence with measles. The telegraph advised that he had died two weeks later.

When Aaron Sage heard the news, he sent the following letter: *"It was hard to receive news that a second brother has died as a result of this miserable war! You really have to say that, because if these soldiers did not have to live in such despicable condi-tions as to break their health, they could hold their own with disease. I am counting the days, dear ones, until I am mustered out of service and can bring father to join you. Unfortunately I must report that the confederates have again taken control of Plymouth. They built a mighty ram, the Albemarle, and the damn thing sank our gunboat, the Southfield. Obviously this is a move we cannot allow to go unchecked. Keep me in your prayers. Love, Aaron"*

Mary Ann Sage had been dead almost six months. I wasn't getting any younger and those kids needed a momma. I swallowed all the courage I could find and walked right into that store. I said to John, *"John, would you look after things around here for a little while? Alfred and I need to take a walk."* Well Alfred looked like someone had planted a sockdologer on him. Outside I proceeded to tell Alfred that I knew he may still be in mourning for his wife, which was under-standable, but that I really didn't want to spend the rest of my life as a widow, and that I had a big heart. *"I was wondering if I were to help you get through this time, and make a home for your children, if you thought in time…well maybe, I mean you might never have sparking feelings towards me, but, maybe you could care for me in a husbandly way?"* There, I had said it. Alfred didn't look up for what I thought seemed like an eternity. When he did, his response was short and to the point, *"I'd be honored."*

On July 23, 1864, Alfred and I were married in my home by Jacob Haskell. My parents, Daniel and Elizabeth Sayer, were the witnesses. Squire and Eliza Smith were there, and Alfred's four oldest children. We announced it to everyone who came in the store the following morning. News in a small community spreads like a wild fire! I moved in with the Sage clan across the corner. And, I guess seeing his momma take the plunge gave Squire courage, because Squire and Eliza were married on September 11, 1864. They lived in the cabin across the creek.

In September, we received congratulations from Aaron: *"I wish you and Mary Ann Buell the very best, dear brother. You have done the right thing. I'm sure she is a wonderful woman. We've taken seven, count them, SEVEN blockaders and tried to sink the confederate Albemarle. She is every bit the match of our ol' Ironsides."*

In October, 1864, newspapers were carrying headlines that the confederates were invading Missouri. General Sterling Price was on the move, while Kansas had been in a lull, thinking their part in the war was nearly over. Even the likes of William Quantrill and Bill Anderson were re-commissioned into the confederate army and told to carry on their side raids, destroying railroads and cutting telegraph wires. Kansas Governor Carney called to arms the Kansas militia. Each man was to bring his own firearms, ammunition, and horse. James's Cavalry unit was sent to the border to patrol from Leavenworth to Paola.

The second regiment of the Kansas State Militia from Shawnee County consisted of ten companies including one 2-gun battery comprised of a 12# brass smoothbore cannon and a 24# Howitzer. Not all regiments of the K.S.M. were sent to the Kansas-Missouri border. Some were to remain on watch within their own areas due to the Plains Indians uprising and the reassigning of various Cavalry units from those posts. The 2nd K.S.M. left for Olathe to prepare for General Price's invading army.

The 2nd regiment of the K.S.M. hadn't anticipated ever having to leave Kansas soil. In fact, many postured that their allegiance was to their state and resisted going beyond the border. However, it became clear that the only thing that stood between Price and some 4,000 Rebels invading Kansas City, was the 2nd K.S.M. If the confederates were to be stopped, they needed to be stopped trying to cross the Big Blue River BEFORE reaching Kansas City.

On October 20, 1864, the 2nd regiment arrived at Hickman Mills, a hamlet of houses and mills in a hilly region where the Santa Fe Trail and the Big Blue River intertwined. German immigrants living in the area assisted the militia in fortifying the river. They felled trees, built barricades along the banks, and dug trenches.

The 11th Cavalry of trained soldiers was sent in first by General Blunt to the west side of the Little Blue River. Price's troops would have to go through them first to get to the Big Blue. Their orders were to detain the confederates as long as possible. The stream was shallow which was to the invaders' advantage. At dawn on October 21, 1864, the Rebels swarmed the stream. The horses slid down the banks on their haunches; riders pursued with guns and sabers drawn. Major Edmund Ross had two different horses shot out from under him during the battle. James Dennitt took a saber through the chest.

All was quiet for two days while the confederate forces regrouped. Their Generals surmised the resistance and decided the "soft spots" were at Byram's Ford and near a farmstead called Mockabee. It was here they would force a crossing of the Big Blue.

Alfred's regiment was located at the Mockabee farm. The militia couldn't differentiate itself from the Rebels who were also largely made up of volunteers who lacked uniforms, so they pinned the red October sumac leaves on their clothing to keep from being mistaken for Rebs. When the Rebels opened fire, they came at them from an orchard and a grove of Locust trees. The militia double-cannistered the Howitzer, sending charges into the grove. The cannon was wheeled around and aimed at Rebs approaching six abreast. When the Rebs were within 100 yards, the cannon was fired, strewing dead bodies and horses. The Rebs were called back.

The farmers were fighting with all the courage they could muster, and for no more military training than most had, were a formidable force Price had not bargained for. The regiment reloaded another double canister. Then came the Rebel cry. Horses lunged over barricades dropping Rebs armed with knives and pistols upon the militia. For 45 minutes, the regiment struggled against an army of confederates many times their number in strength. Finally, the K.S.M. fled to Westport. Casualties were great for both sides, and in the end General Price did not press to cross the Kansas border to take Fort Leavenworth which had been his plan. Instead, he turned his army south. The Union soldiers at Fort Scott were ready.

Wounded soldiers were bandaged in Westport. Before the soldiers were mustered from service, they first built coffins, collected their dead, and brought them home to be buried on Kansas soil in Wyandotte, Kansas.

Newspapers were ablaze with headlines of the 2nd K.S.M. fighting in the *"Gettysburg of the West."* Every woman in Mission Creek waited nervously to see if their loved one was one of the many casualties.

You could see the dust on the horizon as the men on horseback road into the valley that November day. Women shouted from their houses, *"They're home! They're home!"* as they ran to the trail to greet them. Soon families were gathered together, locking arms, crying with sighs of relief. Elizabeth, Ann and I did the same! The children danced in rings around us and cowboy hats were tossed in the air and fluttered to the ground.

Alfred didn't seem as happy as I thought he would be, as happy as the others seemed to be. I noticed John shot him a worrisome glance, but I didn't let on like I noticed. When at last people started for their own homes, and Alfred acknowledged each of the children, he told them to *"Run along and play for a while, so I can talk to Mary Ann."* Mother kind of motioned for the children to go with her, and I handed her Thomas. Alfred slid his arm around my waist as if to support me as I walked. *"Mary Ann, James is dead."* I felt my legs buckle as I looked into Alfred's face in disbelief.

Alfred stayed home with the children that night, as my mother, father and I went to Squire and Eliza's cabin to tell them. Squire was devastated. He kept running his hands through his hair, saying, *"It should have been me!"* Then he laid his head in his arms as he sat at the table and sobbed. We left them alone, so Eliza could comfort him. I, too, needed to be comforted, so I went home and stayed with my parents, instead of to Alfred's bed.

There is little anyone can do to comfort you when you lose a child. You are suppose to die first. When you first hold that baby in your arms, you commit to doing everything in your power to protect them. But life teaches you that we are all part of a much greater plan. When it is your time, it is your time. My family was not the only ones aching in grief. I knew by the time the rest of the soldiers made their way to their homesteads in Mission Creek, Mark and Josephine would be at the side of Mary Copp, ready to face John.

While the militia had been away, Mary had a fire in the flue of the fireplace chimney at the stagecoach station. She could tell there was some kind of obstruction, perhaps a bird's nest that had caught on fire and the station was getting smoky. Not knowing how to get it out, and needing to act quickly, she made the decision to jump on her horse and ride to Mark & Josephine's. Her children, Mary (age 6), Robert (age 5), Ida (age 3) and Hedwig (age 1) were in their beds sleeping. Mark immediately rode with her but could tell after cresting the first hill that the cedar roof on the stone station was ablaze. By the time they arrived, parts of the roof had fallen in, the station was full of black billowy smoke, and all four of the Copp children were dead.

Things seemed rather stiff, or strained between Alfred and me the next several weeks. I don't think it was him, but me. I needed to be loved and held, a degree of affection that our union had not yet accomplished. I know that Alfred was at a loss as to what to do or say. When we were together, we would talk about others in the family. Aaron wrote to congratulate Alfred and John on the successful showdown at the Big Blue. He also crowed that at last they had sunk the Albemarle by exploding a torpedo into her hull. I shared with Alfred that I was very concerned that Squire didn't seem to be handling James's death. He had no desire to even get out of bed. Eliza felt as if he were shutting her out.

I was surprised when Alfred took my hand and said, *"Like his Momma?"* He stood so close to me I could feel his breath against my neck. He then tilted my head upward and kissed me; not just a peck, but a long, hard kiss. That night I felt the closeness that can only come from the union of a husband and wife lying together. I clung to him and didn't want to let go. It had been so long since I had felt the strength of a man at my side. In fact, I wondered as I was falling to sleep if I had ever felt it.

Soon it would be Christmas and I knew it would be important for me to divert the children's attention away from remembering the death of their mother the year before at that time. The older boys and I went out and cut branches of evergreens and tied them together with twine. We looked for the ones with the most berries so that the red birds would visit us frequently and I draped the swag across the front of our home. Elizabeth thought it looked so lovely that she and I made wreaths together and placed them in the windows. After a candle was placed inside the sill, I thought it looked very festive!

Eliza came running down the road, slipping in the snow, and not much on in the way of covering herself from the cold. She was frantic. I saw her from the window before she ever knocked on the door. She didn't have to say anything, I knew. In my gut, with everything in my being, I knew. I ran with her, leaving the children behind without any thought to them, across the ford to her cabin. It was over. Memories of war. The loss of limb. The loss of his brother. Squire lay on the floor, his revolver at his side. No more pain.

Families that wanted to disinter their soldiers at Wyandotte were allowed to do so. The dead could be brought back to their homes. [Gage monument in Topeka Cemetery was erected to memorialize those soldiers from Shawnee County, buried there and elsewhere.] That December, 1864, Alfred, John and Mark took a wagon to Wyandotte, Kansas to bring back James to be buried by his brother, Squire, in the cemetery west of us [Keene] on the Southwest Trail. Friend Henry Harvey presided over a short graveside service. I didn't know if we would ever feel like celebrating on Christmas again. Shortly after the service for my sons, the Harvey's left our area, which was a loss for my family spiritually.

A dispatch sent to newspaper offices throughout the states reported that President Lincoln had received a unique Christmas present—a telegram from General Sherman:

Dec. 22, 1864
His Excellency President Lincoln,
I beg to present you as a Christmas gift the city of Savannah, with 150 heavy guns and plenty of ammunition, and also about 25,000 bales of cotton.
W. T. Sherman

In January, John Copp visited with Mark Sage about where he and Mary may go from there. He told Mark they had no intentions to rebuild the stage station. In fact, he didn't want anything to ever be built there again. As the government continued to re-shuffle where the Indian tribes could live, John Copp thought there would be a future on Mill Creek when the Pottawatomie Reserve opened

[Later named Paxico]. Until that time, he thought he'd just farm. He and Mary would need some time to let their hearts heal. He gave his blessing to someone else, including Mark, to build a new station as one would be needed.

Mark knew he had more than he could handle after having acquired another 160 acres of land the year before. He and Josephine were building another house, and would be cultivating the land for crops. Besides, his skills were being heavily sought after to build stone bridges in the area. Alfred, on the other hand, had already talked to Mark about intending to build another place for us that Spring so that we would have a home of our own apart from John and Elizabeth, where, with all the children, the living quarters were becoming cramped.

When Mark told Alfred what John Copp had said, and that he was not intending to follow through on the opportunity, Alfred told Mark that if he were to build a lay-over station on the land he had bought for Samuel, it would be close to the store and good for business. Alfred had inherited the land from Samuel's estate and needed to make improvements to it in order to keep it.

I knew my father, Daniel Sayer, would be willing to help us build, but when we told mother and him about the idea, my father had another suggestion. His thinking was that since their land was right on the corner of the trail's bend where Mission Creek could be forded, it would make more sense to build the station there, plus it would be closer to the store. After Samuel's land had been held for the five years, they would convey the deeds to each other's land and make the switch complete. In the meantime, if something were to happen, it really wouldn't matter, because I would stand to inherit from both of them as Daniel's only daughter and Alfred's wife. So it was agreed. Mark and John agreed to help, too. After the station was built, they'd either dismantle the cabin and rebuild it on the neighboring claim, or they'd continue to live in the cabin behind the Inn while building another stone house to the north.

We signed a contract with the Southwestern Stage Company which was owned and operated by Henry Tisdale of Lawrence and J. W. Parker of Atchison.

We decided to call our place "*The Sage Inn*" because we would rent three rooms on the upper floor. The main floor would have a back parlor, and the front room would be used for dining. We could access this room from the kitchen downstairs and we had two rooms for our sleeping quarters off of the kitchen. The land was naturally stair-stepped: the creek, the bottoms where my folks had built, and the land that was level with the trail. We decided to take advantage of the lay of the land by building out from the stair-step. By squaring up the side of the hill, we had the east wall of the lower level already, and built outward to the west. Being tucked against the side of the hill offered the same kind of protection as a dug-out. Once the lower level was built, the rest went up easily because the next floor was also at ground level. After what had happened at the Copp's place, Alfred didn't put any fireplaces in the Inn, instead he ordered parlor stoves and we burned coal.

Before the Inn was completely built, Alfred went to Topeka and sent a telegram to his father, Samuel. Aaron had been mustered from the service March 11, 1865, at Hilton Head, South Carolina, after his naval expedition closed the last seaport available to the confederates, Fort Fisher at Wilmington.

On April 7, 1865, General Lee surrendered to General Grant, the Civil War had finally ended. There was one final parting shot, however, before this part of our lives ended. On April 14, 1865, the following week, President Abraham Lincoln was assassinated. The opening of the Sage Inn was bittersweet in a country that mourned, but it will be forever memorable that the Sage Inn opened the same month and year that President Lincoln was shot. Aaron and Samuel Sage left the turmoil back East and were our first guests at the Inn.

I was very pleased when Aaron began courting my daughter-in-law who lived behind us in the cabin across the creek. I assumed that she would go back to living with her family at the ferry crossing, but she did not. Her sister, Isabel Haskell, lived here and she wanted to keep the land and cabin she had inherited from my son's estate. Still I worried about her being alone. She wasn't that far away, but in the country, a few feet can seem like miles when a crisis occurs!

The building of the railroad across Kansas kept Kansas from experiencing true peace. The great iron horse that scattered the buffalo further antagonized the Indians on the plains. Bands of them appeared without warning and many settlers were killed. Edmund Ross stayed in the Cavalry, headquartered out of Fort Riley. In July, 26 members of the 11th Kansas Regiment, including Sergeant A. J. Custer, escorted a train to Platt Bridge where they were surrounded and attacked by 1,500 Indians. They ran out of ammunition after three hours. The Indians bound them with telegraph wire and burned them to death. Major Ross, James Bassett, and John St. John mustered out of service with the Cavalry in September, 1865. Edmund and Fannie Ross decided to move back to Lawrence to again run a newspaper.

John and Mark were both earning quite a reputation for being good stone masons. They built their own shop/residence on 1st Street in Topeka, between Jackson and Van Buren. It worked out well for them that in 1865 Merifield Vicory moved to the area and opened a quarry on the land that had been occupied by the Massasoit Indians until they moved on. If limestone was ordered for a job in Topeka, Mr. Vicory would load the limestone in his wagon one day, drive it to his home, then get up at four in the morning the next day and head for Topeka, unload it, spend the night, drive back to Mission Creek and repeat the process.

Before the year 1865 was over, we had our first bridge across Mission Creek. The Sage brothers landed a job in Topeka to work on the first Shawnee County courthouse which would have a limestone foundation and much limestone architectural accents. Mark's abilities with making arches was needed as arc-pediments were desired. From that point on, the Sage brothers had steady work in Topeka. They laid twelve foot slabs of limestone for sidewalks on Kansas Avenue, built a house for Dr. Crane [Topeka Cemetery office] with Mark's signature arc-window in front, and were chosen, along with my father, Daniel Sayer, to be stone masons on the Kansas State Capitol.

My father was concerned about taking the job as he had been so busy the past year working on the Sage Inn and the bridge over Mission Creek, but mother said that most of her time was needed to help me with the kids or with guests, so that there really wasn't any rush to get another house built—it would be the NEXT project!

The first wedding at the Sage Inn was set for December 25, 1865. Aaron Sage would wed Eliza Smith Dennitt. Only a year ago, I thought I would never be able to again face the holiday, and here I was happily hanging my evergreen swags and adding ribbons and candles to the parlor. I truly had grown to love my daughter-in-law. She and Aaron helped to fill the void in my heart. Aaron was a delightful man. So happy and charismatic. He had a great sense of humor, as all the Sage brothers did. And, he was gifted at playing the violin. After the ceremony, we pushed away the chairs and danced until late in the night. It was the happiest Christmas I can remember.

There was a boon in Shawnee County during the years 1866 to 1876. Crops were good on the farms, log cabins and dug-outs were abandoned for stone homes, the market grew in Topeka as its population doubled, and the new eastern division of the Union Pacific Railway would forever change the way commerce was done. The railway company was allowed to build tracks from the Missouri River west. By 1864, the railway tracks were completed to Lawrence and the first passenger train to Topeka came January 1, 1866.

We received a telegraph that Arthur, Alfred's oldest brother, and his wife, Kezia, had decided to move to Kansas.

"With news of the railroad going all the way to Topeka, dear brothers, I can surely ROUGH IT out West! Now with father gone, we find we're actually lonely. We will see you soon. If only that younger brother hadn't been so hot to trot, we could have come to the wedding!"

In February, 1866, Arthur, Kezia, and their four children: Ann (age 19), Sara (age 17), Emily (age 15), and Albert (age 13) were picked up at the Union Pacific Train Depot in Topeka. John Sage had been offered a goodly sum of money for the large stone and frame house that had served as a divided residence for he and Elizabeth, and Alfred and me. James Gillis, who was a bachelor, had agreed to move to Dover to teach school. He liked the proximity to the school, and was willing to buy both he and Alfred's land around it, so that he and Elizabeth and their children could move to Topeka. John did not like working away from the family and felt that his fortune lie in his abilities as a mason, rather than a farmer. He said Mark may want to keep one foot in each door, but he did not. Alfred understood, but of all his brothers, of course, John and he were closest and it would be difficult to see them move. Now, with Arthur's family arriving, John was very troubled about what to do. He had let Arthur's family live in the half that Alfred and me had moved out of.

Aaron, who was closer to Arthur, thought he had the perfect solution and said he would approach Arthur about building a cabin north of he and Eliza. Aaron told Arthur that he and Eliza would be willing to enter into an agreement for them to live on the north 80 acres of their place. He explained that when the Civil War ended, the Homestead Act of 1862 was amended so that the five year requirement to get the deed to your land was offset by the amount of time a man served in the military. Squire, then Eliza as Squire's widow, had lived on the land since January, 1864. Squire was in the Cavalry for 15 months, so in a little over two years, they would be able to sell the whole 160 acres to Arthur and build their own place elsewhere. Aaron said he didn't know much about farming, so his intention was to raise chickens for their eggs and plant berries to take to market, so he really had no need for the additional land. Then he also told Arthur, that John was hoping to act on an offer he had been given for the house they were staying in. Well, Arthur couldn't act fast enough. His timing had been off, the last thing he wanted to do was put anyone out.

John and Alfred sold the building and the land to James Gillis, but exempted the cabin and land where Alfred had the store. John and Elizabeth moved to Topeka with their children, Samuel, Maddie, and their new baby boy, Cyrus, who John had already started calling "Mack." Mark and Josephine had also had a baby girl in 1866, Rose; and Aaron and Eliza had their first baby, a son, George.

Arthur, Aaron, Alfred and James Bassett worked swiftly and put up a cabin just north of Aaron and Eliza's. Well let me tell you, if it wasn't love at first sight, it was close to it. The minute Arthur's oldest daughter, Ann, laid eyes on James Bassett, she was in love! In November, they were married. As a wedding gift,

Arthur and Kezia offered to extend their home to connect with Aaron and Eliza's, creating a middle cabin and getting a jump-start on building a larger home for themselves. The old cabin that James lived in wasn't suitable for their daughter, apparently. True it was very primitive, and small, but we older settlers were just thankful to even have a dug-out of our own.

A year after Senator James Lane was re-elected in 1865, the populace was astounded to learn that he took his own life. In some people's eyes, Lane had become as fanatical as John Brown, to the point of driving himself mad. Edmund Ross, who had only been back at the paper in Lawrence less than a year, was chosen for Lanes replacement. The reconstruction process for the re-admission of confederate states to the union created political turmoil. Someone like Ross, who as a journalist followed the political process minutely, was a good choice. Ross, being a man of principles, voted his conscience, and was the one vote that kept Congress from impeaching President Johnson, whom Ross felt was being railroaded by radical politicians attempting to further their own agenda.

Porter and Alwilda Cook were settlers from Pennsylvania who bought farm land in Mission Creek after the war. They were religious people, and after the Harvey family left our area, would sometimes join our family in prayer and Bible study. We particularly enjoyed meeting in their home, as Alwilda had brought an organ from back East, the first musical instrument that I was aware of, in our area. When she played, it was almost like going to heaven! As our community continued to grow, it became apparent to me that we needed to have some kind of "organized" worship, rather than having tiny groups meeting hit or miss up and down Mission Creek.

Father St. John and the Methodists were busily working on ministering to the influx of Negroes into Topeka after the Civil War. They had plans for building a church where the Negro immigrants could attend worship together [St. John's African Methodist Episcopal Church—1868]. Father St. John had started a Sunday school in Auburn, and that community had already built a Methodist Church and a Baptist Church. Ultimately, though, I think I identified more with the Baptists as I was somewhat familiar with the Baptist Mission's work on the Kansas River and it reminded me of the Quaker's ministry to the Shawnee Indians.

I called on the Auburn Baptists to learn how to go about starting a Sunday School in Mission Creek. Elder Raymond told me he would be willing to meet with followers every other week on a Sunday afternoon. I knew if I could get the various families to attend, there would be too many to meet in a house, but God provided the best place, a grove of lovely trees on our land straight north of us.

The best way to get something started is to just pick a date and DO IT! So I picked a Spring day in 1867 as the day our Baptist Sunday School would begin, then I spent several weeks driving the spring wagon to all the different homes in the valley inviting them to Sunday School. When I called on Porter Cook, I told him, *"I'm going to get the people there, you're going to be the Superintendent!"* Well, naturally, he tried to beg off, but I knew he would do it for me.

I thought God was sending more for me and my mother to bear than we could handle the summer of 1867. Indeed, if we had not started our church, and had the support of all those good people, I don't know what would have happened. Mark Sage drove a wagon from Topeka to the Sage Inn. Not unusual, I thought for Mark to stop off and visit with Alfred, but it was unusual for him to park the wagon at the Inn and walk that far to the store. I saw from the window of the Inn, Alfred rush out of the store and across the street to the Inn with Mark right behind him. They stopped at the wagon where Mark pulled back the canvass to show Alfred the contents in the bed. Alfred quickly covered it back up.

When Alfred and Mark walked inside, the first thing he said was, *"Where's your mother?"*

I said, *"She's in her cabin out back."*

Then Mark interjected, *"I think you need to sit down, Mary Ann."*

"Just say it!" I think I said to him abruptly, because by now I could feel my body trembling, sensing what Mark's response would be.

"Mary Ann, your father fell from the scaffolding while working on the capitol."

Oh, dear God, first my sons, now my father. Daniel Sayer may not have been my natural father, but he was the only father I had ever known, and I absolutely adored him.

"Mary Ann, do you want me to go with you to tell your mother?" Alfred asked.

"No," I said, *"You and Mark do whatever you need to do with father's body, and I will go tell mother."* The first funeral service held at the Sage Inn was for Daniel Sayer, age 67.

In 1868, all kinds of things happened in Mission Creek. Mark and Josephine had another son, Walter; Aaron and Eliza had a son, too, William, but sadly, he was stillborn. Alfred's youngest sister, Elizabeth, her husband, Ted Stock, and two children, Frank and Mattie, moved here, making the migration of the Sage family complete.

The Stocks bought land along Ross's creek, on south of the Ross family's settlement. Elizabeth was scared out of her wits the first time that an Indian happened by. Seeing that some new folks had settled there, he peeked in the window. To avoid the glare, he took his blanket and brought it up over his head and held it to each side of the window frame. I imagine that would frighten the best of us, even we early settlers! Elizabeth grabbed a butcher knife and hid under the bed with the children. Ted said she didn't know how long they stayed there, but she hid until Ted came inside.

Alfred had the chance to sell his store to Harvey Loomis. Harvey negotiated with James Gillis to finish purchasing the front part of his land because he hoped to construct a new mercantile. Mr. Gillis really didn't have need for as much land as he had bought from John and Alfred. He had a few ponies and converted half of the building into a barn for them. He had a nephew, T. K. Tomson, that wound up starting a livery there.

Alfred stopped running the store. We had 335 acres of land, a barn that was forty foot square, cattle stables, granary, the grist mill, the inn, raised sheep for their wool, pigs for meat, and had 100–200 heads of cattle most of the time. Instead he thought his priority should be to build the stone house for my mother that father had always promised her.

My mother's house was built about a half-mile north of us on our land by the beautiful grove of trees where Sunday school gathered. However, our church had grown to the point that we were ready to put the building of a church to a vote. Alfred's sisters' families, the Mains and the Stocks, also joined the church with Alfred, me, and my mother; as did several others in the community. Ann and Simon had nine children [Addie and Albert were born around 1864, 1866], and Ann would joke with me about how many more new members did I need? *"The Baptist Society,"* as we called ourselves, met throughout the winter in the log school house on Sundays. By the end of the year, Mark Sage had built us a new stone Baptist Church across the road to the east of the Sage Inn. I told him that if he wasn't careful, that Holy place may rub off on him. Alfred's brothers were not too keen on religion, but work was work.

Aaron found out that even the best laid plans, sometimes don't pan out the way you think they will. Arthur and Kezia didn't like living on the bottoms, so when Ann and James built a home to the east of St. John's, they, too, moved. There was a problem with their cabins flooding whenever Mission Creek rose. We had the same problems, which was why Alfred wanted mother to live some place other than the cabin in back, and why we chose to leave the bottom floor of the Sage Inn dirt! I didn't have to have the wide-plank yellow pine on every floor. Arthur became a grocer for Craigue & Sons in Topeka, and also sold farm implements.

People always ask me how I like running the Sage Inn, and I tell them, *"It's a lot of work!"* I don't know how I would do it without my mother and the children. Mother's in her seventies and does most of the cooking. She's spry as a cricket and everyone around calls her *"Granny Sayer."* After her house was finished, Alfred decided we should make the cabin in back a *"summer kitchen,"* or where we do the cooking and have the fire. That way if we would have a fire, we'd have a much better likelihood of not also losing the Inn. We use the underground room for cold storage for things like milk, cheese and butter. Our daughter, Maggie, carries the trays of food from the kitchen, up the back stairway to the dining room, where she serves guests. Afterwards, she clears the tables and hauls the dirty dishes downstairs where she washes them in the dry sink.

The younger boys, James and Dudley, help me with the cleaning. They sweep floors, empty chamber pots, trim wicks and refill lamp oil, scrub the soot off the ceilings, air out the feather beds, clean windows, and do anything else that I need help with, like gathering vegetables from the garden or picking up walnuts from the trees on our land. Willie, or "Bill", (now that he's older he prefers to be called Bill,) and Squire help with tending to the livestock, pumping water from the wells (we have two), plowing the fields for the vegetables, and for the corn we grow for silage.

Stages get generally about three miles to the hour so the horses are driven at an all-out pace. As the older boys would see the stage turn the corner at Granny's, they'd round up the grazing horses, so the stage would have four fresh ones to continue on the next leg of the route.

After Eliza received the deed to their property, she and Aaron sold the land west of the Sage Inn to George "Louis" and Louisa Wirth. Aaron and Eliza purchased land to the west and down the road past the Berryman's. They chose to build above the cliff, and thanks to Mark and his bridges, they were able to do so at this point.

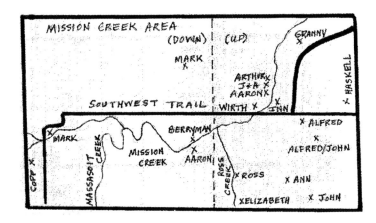

The Wirths were very nice people. Louis wanted the location precisely because it was behind the Sage Inn where the stagecoach laid over and traded out horses. We had built a barn and corral [Dover fire station] where we kept extra horses. George wanted to convert the 3-room cabins on the land into a blacksmith shop. The Wirths fit right into the community. They joined our Baptist church, and we even had them stay at the Inn as our guests for a while during construction of their own stone house on the other side of the creek. During that time, Louis and Louisa were our first baptisms in our church. They were baptized in Mission Creek behind the Inn. Alfred provided a lumber wagon with hay and blankets to keep them warm so they wouldn't get sick from exposure. Then they went back to the Inn to change clothes and we all celebrated! The Wirths were only on the land for five years before there was a fire in the blacksmith shop. When they moved, Alfred purchased all the ground west of the creek.

By 1870 there was enough commerce going on in our tiny hamlet, and travelers passing through on the Southwest Trail, that those of us living up Mission Creek thought it was long overdue that we give ourselves a name. The name agreed upon was *"Dover"* but who was to receive credit for that became a bone of contention. Jacob Haskell said it was HIS idea because he had come from Dover, New Hampshire, which ruffled Alfred's feathers, since HE had been here FIRST and said the name was after Dover, England.

"Just look around at your friends and neighbors, Jacob. How many of them are from England and how many of them are from New Hampshire?!" Rarely have I ever seen Alfred get hot under the collar, but he was then.

James Bassett piped up and said, *"Well, I was in Dover, Arkansas during the war, maybe we'll name it for that Dover!"* to which everyone had a good chuckle and it broke the tension. To this day, if you ask someone who named Dover, some will say Sage, some will say Haskell.

In 1870, Mark and Josephine had another baby boy, Mark. He came out screaming with his face all distorted. Mark said, *"He's going to be an ugly one, just like me, so, Josie, we're going to have to call this one Mark."* Mark was always saying things like that. One time there was a contest in Wabaunsee County where they wanted a photo of the ugliest man in the county. Mark sent his own picture in! Josephine could have killed him. He was more rugged looking than his brothers, but he wasn't ugly by a long shot. Mark just loved to make jokes, even at his own expense. Ultimately, they wound up calling Mark, Jr., *"Arc."* Mark said, *"that way they'll always know you're one of MY boys."*

The North Topeka Baptist liked our church so much, that they hired Mark to build a stone church for them. Mark Sage literally had all the work he could ever want.

Little George, Aaron and Eliza's son, finally had a playmate. Eliza gave birth to a healthy baby boy, Fred, in 1870. Incidentally, Eliza's sister, Sara, married Merifield Vicory, a confirmed bachelor. We didn't think he or James Gillis, either one, would ever get married.

Alfred's father, Samuel, died December 9, 1871, of old age. He was 96 years old. Since coming to Dover, he first stayed with Alfred and I; then moved in with Aaron and Eliza when they built their new home west of town. Father Samuel was buried in the Topeka Cemetery, as a burial plot had been given to the Sage Brothers as partial payment for the home and carriage house they built for Dr. Crane.

Simon and Ann Main's sons, Morris and Frank, worked for Alfred in the grist/saw mill south of the Inn. As they got older, and started taking a greater interest in their own livelihood, they said, *"Uncle Alf, why don't you change to a steam engine and update this old mill? We've been reading about how efficient it is to operate with steam."* Well, Uncle Alf, decided that those boys may know what they were talking about, so he made a proposal to them. He told them that if they would determine what was needed and order the equipment, he'd finance the change over.

After everything was done, Uncle Alf surprised the boys by telling them that he would sell the mill to them on contract. Alfred said, *"It'll just be one less thing for me to have to worry about."*

Alfred could never stay out of being in the thick of things, though, and before I knew it, he was back involved in the mercantile business. Cary Snyder had built a general store shortly after Harvey Loomis had bought out Alfred. Now, within a couple of years, Snyder was ready to sell, and who did he want to sell it to? That's right.

Aaron and Eliza had another boy, that makes three. His name is Clark. Aaron has planted a wonderful orchard and is doing very well for himself raising and selling produce in the Topeka market. [Aaron later was one of the incorporaters of the Dover State Bank and was Vice President for many years.]

In 1872, Arthur and Kezia's daughter, Emily, died from exposure [pneumonia]. She was 21 years old and just beginning to start her married life.

Harry Perkins moved to Dover in 1873. He moved here from Notting Hill, London, England via New York. Alfred took an immediate liking to Harry since he had traveled to Kansas the same route as he, albeit 20 years later! Harry had been a successful plasterer in England where he learned how to make beautiful ornate ceilings and crown molding. Most people could not afford to put something like that in their homes, the real business was where towns were developing. His intent was to come to Topeka and work on all the new commercial buildings going up as the town grew. In conversation with Alfred, he mentioned that he just knew that after he had a first job under his belt, people would see his work and be so impressed that they would hire him as well. Alfred had a great idea. Why don't you put those fancy ceilings in the Sage Inn and that'll be my gift to Mary Ann for our tenth anniversary.

I was stunned when Mr. Perkins was finished, because before he was done, all I could focus on was what a mess he was making and how difficult it was to work around him. But, Alfred was right. It made the perfect anniversary present. Those ceilings were prettier than any wedding cake. I watched Mr. Perkins make them, too, just like decorating a cake. He'd make the pretty flowers on flat surfaces, wait until they were completely dry, then use "frosting" to affix them to the ceiling. I'm sure the ceilings at the Sage Inn will be remembered long after I'm dead and forgotten. We had many visitors from Topeka as a result. I told Alfred that we were Mr. Perkins' salesman's sample.

Just between you and me, I think the real reason that Alfred made such a big deal out of our anniversary was out of guilt! You see, he spent $2,000 on a Percheron-Norman stallion which he had a Mr. Dunham import for him. I couldn't say too much since Alfred wasn't the type to usually spend money on himself, but $2000!!

Between the years of 1872 and 1874, three million buffalo were slaughtered for profit. We had become a wasteful society. Each buffalo brought $3 a head. Large herds that were once in the west part of the Mission Creek valley became extinct. One way to force a people from the land is to take away their livelihood. The Indian tribes moved on. You seldom saw a Kansa after 1873, as they moved down to Oklahoma.

Perhaps there was a just irony in that in 1874, the Lord sent a plague upon us equal to anything the people of Egypt had ever seen. Chinch bugs wiped out wheat field, after wheat field. And it wasn't just chinch bugs—grasshoppers and Rocky Mountain locusts!! Chinch bugs would strip the rye from the wheat; grasshoppers and locusts would kill everything else: fruit trees, corn fields, you name it! About mid-day you'd see hordes of winged creatures, looked like storm clouds, moving in. They wouldn't leave until there wasn't a living thing left. Even worse, we knew that they would likely lay eggs that would hatch a bumper crop in the

Spring. Planting was late in 1875 as the farmers attempted to starve out the parasites.

This plague wiped out the mercantile business for both Mr. Loomis and for Alfred. There was no money to be made. In fact, we were back once again to how Alfred first started the store, as distribution agents for government relief. Shawnee County sold bonds to raise money to help the farmers. Right in the middle of this terrible misfortune, Aaron and Eliza had a baby girl—at last! Her name was Minnie and the only ray of hope we had seen in months.

Our church had its first wedding! W. T. and Polly Berryman saw their daughter, Elizabeth, marry Israel Eddy. Elizabeth lost her mother, Hannah, when she was eight years old and W. T. had her go live with the Olds family for a couple of years. She then returned to look after the house for W. T. and her brothers. When she was a little thing I remember her wading in the creek and singing, *"I want to be an angel and with the angels stand, with a crown upon my forehead and a harp within my hand."* She was the cutest little thing. I'm glad she found happiness.

We didn't keep in as close of touch with John's as I had hoped we would. But that was more our fault, than theirs. The stage station was a 24 hour a day, 7 days a week commitment. John and Elizabeth's farm was west of Topeka, considerably closer than Dover. [Around 10th & Gerald, 1 block west of Wanamaker. They later moved to Richland, Kansas.] Elizabeth had three more boys, Edwin, Charley and Earl. John and Mark continued to work together on projects in Topeka. They built a commercial building in the first block of Kansas Avenue down by the river. [Given the architecture and proximity to the building on 1st, thought to be the body shop below Kansas Avenue Bridge.] Mark and Josephine had two more sons, Will and Edgar around 1874–76; Aaron and Eliza had another son, Charlie in 1876.

Just as the community rose to be bigger and stronger after the drought, the same held true after the plague. The Southwestern Stage Company was purchased by Root Brothers Transfer Company of Wichita in 1878. They had lines that went as far east as Emporia which was the western terminus for the Southwestern. They continued to expand, knowing that it would still be some time before the railroad would be accessible to small towns throughout Kansas. In the 1870's, the stagecoach was still the primary means of transportation for most Kansans.

We contracted with them to expand and to continue to operate as a stage stop for a minimum of five years, renewable at the end of that time. Everything was done up nice and legal with a set of rules and regulations as to what we agreed to do as agents for the stagecoach company. Way-bills and tickets had to be accounted for, the time of arrival for the stage and the name of the driver put on the way-bills. We had to build our own blacksmith shop and livery because the horses couldn't be shod or the coach repaired except by a station agent.

Our son, Squire, was old enough to handle the mercantile, and Bill, the oldest, looked after all the horses and livery. We hired a smithy from Bohemia, Charles Lambert, or as others got to know him, "Old Dutch Charley." He was hard for others to understand but he did good work. He preferred to sleep in the stable with his horse.

Two tenant farmers by the name of Byron Baird and Joseph McLatchey helped reinforce the Southwest Trail about four miles northeast of the Inn by building a stone wall from rocks they picked up in the neighboring farm fields. The curve was becoming hard to traverse with all the ruts, so they worked on smoothing it out and shoring up the sides so that the coach wouldn't tip.

We built onto the Sage Inn so that the size was doubled. When finished, it had over 3,000 square feet, three floors. We set it up so that you came in the first door, the old dining room, if you wanted to check into the Inn for the night. You came into the second and third doors of the new addition if you had stage business or wanted to get a bite to eat.

The middle door was for stage business. You walked in and there was a long counter where we processed mail, freight, sold tickets for the stage and so on.

Indians were fairly scarce in these parts after 1873 when the Kansa were moved to Oklahoma. It was the cowboy that Alfred had a real problem with as they came through with their firearms loaded. Usually those with a quick draw, had a quick temper. In a lot of ways, you had to be more cautious of them than you ever were of the Indians, because they were sneaky. You never knew if one of these guys would wind up being a highway man [robber] or not, so Alfred exercised his authority as station agent by asking that they remove their guns and holsters while on the premises. He hammered iron spikes into the wall of the station, where we always had someone on duty, and draped the firearms on these pegs until the man left.

The highway man may be a passenger on a stage, and after finding out information about others on the stage, if he found someone had money, he'd find a way to personally mark the stage, according to some predetermined method agreed upon with partners down the line. This was called horse telegraphy. That way, they'd know which stages to hold up. The same was true if a strong box was picked up from the station agent.

Truly, there were a lot of gun fights in the 1870's; things got worse after the war. When Mark helped move the Copp family from the old station, they found the skeleton of a man under the floor boards of the livery stable. John Copp was as stunned as Mark! Well, it turns out he wasn't shot, the examiner said he died from a blow to the head. The skull had been fractured in three places. He speculated by a bullwhip. And yet, nobody ever came through looking for the poor soul. One of the stagecoach drivers, Billy Brooks, used to be a gunfighter, and brags about it. I wish they'd be more careful about the men they hire. I guess everyone deserves another chance in life. The drivers all have to sign an agreement that they will not engage in drunkenness, reckless driving, polling passengers, or any other civil disobedience. I keep a watchful eye out, especially for Maggie.

We made the south room into a dining hall. Maggie, at age 16, is quite the pretty young woman. Every cowboy that comes through gets a crush on her, but I think she has her eye on the Glanville boy. The deputy sheriff at Auburn tracked a Negro all the way to Wamego, Kansas after Harrison White's daughter was raped. In the meantime, one of the farmers in the area saw a black man, and after hearing about Miss White being raped, shot him. The wrong man paid dearly for the crime. When you live out in the country, you maintain a certain amount of suspicion about every stranger.

We've got two more big bedrooms upstairs that holds another four beds. We also had a six foot copper soaking tub specially made and put in a small room up there for people to rinse the dirt off from the stage ride. They are most grateful, after being shaken to mortal pieces and covered with dust. A good soaking seems like heaven! We usually carry two buckets at a time full of water drawn from the well. Then we heat the water on top of a parlor stove in the southeast bedroom at the top of the stairs. After the tub is filled, the copper keeps the water hot so that everyone has warm water. Then the last person pulls the plug and the water goes down a drain pipe all the way to the ground level where we collect it for filling the stove reservoir in the kitchen. Very efficient!

The room below the station expanded our own sleeping quarters which had been under the first dining area, our front parlor. And the room under the dining hall, we've left unfinished, but now we have a room available for future purposes. For now the dogs like to go in there where its cool, so we put some straw down and let them burrow around.

At the same time we had all this expansion going on at the Sage Inn, things were changing over at our old place. James Gillis sold to his nephew, T. K. Tomson who had big plans for raising new thorobred cattle called, Shorthorns. Lloyd and Fannie Knapp had started a farm *"Spring Glen"* six miles northwest of Dover and they, too, were into raising this new breed. Since they had become members of our church, I had learned that Shorthorns were bred to be a good beef cow for slaughter, but they also give milk and butter while they're being grazed. Tomson added onto and finished building a frame Victorian house his uncle had started next door to the stone and frame building. Then he tore the old framing off of the stone building and turned it into a barn for his prize cows.

It was a big surprise to us when Alfred's nephew, John William Sage, moved to Dover from New York the following year (1879). John William was George and Mary Guppy Sage's son, Alfred's half-brother from Samuel's marriage to Sharlot Hayden [Descendants were Priddy-Firestone families]. It was a surprise because his two sisters, Charlotte and Hannah, still lived in New York. John William's brother, Henry Valentine, had moved from New York after the Civil War, however, and was building bridges for the Wabash Railroad in Missouri. John W. was still a newly wed. He and Sarah Satterley had only been married for three months when they came to Dover.

Maggie was the first of our children to get married. She married William Glanville who worked with Joe and Alfred Main at Haskell's cheese factory. The cheese was made in a building on Jacob Haskell's land back in behind Haskell's stone house, but purchases were made at the home. We had Maggie and William's wedding at the Sage Inn, just like when Uncle Aaron got married. She made a beautiful bride. I think Mary Ann, her mother, was with her in spirit, and Mary Ann, her other mother, was very proud of the young woman she'd become.

It was around 1880, when a newly married couple by the name of Isaac and Sara Lister moved to Dover from up around Mayetta, Kansas. They stopped at the Inn to see if we would lease the Wirth house that stood empty across the creek. [Later on, this same couple would have a little girl named, Eva, that would come over and help Alfred with housekeeping at the Sage Inn after Mary Ann died.]

John William liked our town so well that he convinced Henry Valentine and Emma McDowell Sage to move from Missouri to Dover in 1880. By now there are so many Sage's in Dover, no one can keep straight who's who and who was born to who!

Other new comers between 1876 and 1880 were John and Elizabeth Todd, George and Emma Kemble, and J.W. Winter and his mother. J.W. was 22 years old and Alfred suggested to Morris and Frank Main that they hire J.W. to work at the mill. Alfred was always trying to help someone get a start. J. W. wound up being our nephew-in-law because he married Morris and Frank's sister, Libby, in 1882.

Mark and Josephine also had their last son, Tom, in 1882.

I guess I really should have expected it. Every day since the Sage Inn was built, my mother walked the half-mile from her place to the north, to the Inn to cook meals for guests. One day she didn't come. I sent Bill down to Granny's house to see. She could have fallen, I reasoned. When Bill returned, he said, *"Ma, Granny's dead. She's sleeping peacefully in her bed."* I don't remember my mother being sick a day, and she worked right up until the day she died. Granny Sayer was 87 years old when she died in 1883.

John and Ellen Scott moved to Dover in 1883. John was likely attracted to the area for the same reason that the Sage's had been—limestone! It was so plentiful, you could drive down any trail and see it laying in the fields. John was also a stone mason, but being younger than the Sage brothers, had learned how to work with concrete. He was very precise with the rock-saw, too. Alfred once said he hadn't seen that type of precision since Daniel Sayer was alive (which made me feel good).

Well, just like Alfred did with Harry Perkins, he gave John Scott a project that would show off his abilities. The dining room bay windows were added to the Sage Inn by John Scott right after he came to Dover. The cornice is a blocked saw-tooth, for lack of a better way of describing it. You can imagine how long it would take to make just the right piece to go around those windows because if one of the tiny blocks would chip, he'd have to start over. The windows bring in so much light to the dining room, they are the focal point of the room. I'd see John out there sawing away, and I wondered was it really worth that much trouble? In the end, I could only say, yes indeed!

In 1884, Alfred and I became grandparents. Maggie and William had a boy, Oscar. When you become a grandparent, it's like you finally realize your whole life's purpose. Alfred and I loved little Oscar. I made Alfred order him one of those new tricycles that even had ball bearings in the pedals and wire wheels. It was too big for him, but I knew he'd grow into it! Then for the next two years, Maggie had Mary Etta (1885) and Carolyn Jane (1887). These were the first little girls I had gotten to spoil since Maggie was a youngster.

We were saddened when the Sage matriarch, Ann Main, passed away in 1885. She was born after Arthur, and had been not only a big sister, but also a mother figure for the Sage family after Elizabeth Davis Sage died in 1860. Ann was the first person to be buried in the newly chartered cemetery in Dover on land where it all began, the original claim of John and Alfred, where their first cabin was built.

Normally, I forget about Alfred being younger than me, but when I'm wanting to slow down and be a grandma, and he's ready to start a new business, it becomes apparent. After Ann's death, Alfred began construction of a new mercantile south of the Inn. I told him he could do as he liked, but I really wished he had decided to take life a little easier.

Our son, James married Lizzie Younker in 1888. Lizzie was the daughter of Bowman and Agnes Younker at Keene. I don't know if Bill and Squire are ever going to tie the knot! The following year, James and Lizzie had a little girl, Ethel.

Our daughter, Maggie, had continued to help me work at the Sage Inn, even after the little ones were born. They played outside most of the time, and stayed downstairs when it was too cold for them to do so. In March of 1889, Maggie began developing a really bad cough. I doctored her with hot compresses for fear that she'd gotten sick from exposure [pneumonia] to the cold winter wind. When her cough wasn't getting any better, I insisted that she go to see Dr. Carson. After examining her, Dr. Carson told her he thought she had consumption [tuberculosis]. Dr. Carson said that he had been reading some journals wherein doctors debated about what they thought caused consumption. The most recent thought was that it came from the mucus of another sick person, and with Maggie handling so many dishes and towels that have come in contact with others, she probably got it from a guest at the Sage Inn. The only prescribed care was rest and lots of fresh air. He recommended that she sleep some place where the air could circulate around her and aid her breathing.

Maggie did not yet realize that she was with child, but soon enough we knew that her condition was even further weakened by carrying a baby. Dr. Carson could not predict whether her body would be able to fight off the disease. I told Alfred that Maggie wasn't going to get rest working for us, nor would she get rest taking care of three little ones while she was with child. She needed to stay with us where I could look after her and the children.

Alfred turned to John Scott for assistance. He told John that he needed to put on a sleeping porch with lots of windows, up high, where it could get the breezes, not down low tucked into the hillside. We needed to devise a way to support the weight of a porch, without adding on even more to the downstairs. John said he could make limestone pillars from segments fitted together with an iron rod in the center. They would look nice and also bear the load. So after John had the pillars finished, we built a porch out of timber with six windows on the southwest side of the Sage Inn.

We kept the windows open all of the time. Maggie had a bed out on the porch. We also had another bed, away from hers a bit, where the babes could take naps. Emily was born in January 1890. For three years, we watched our daughter struggle with consumption. Sometimes she would cough so hard, she spat up blood. She'd say, *"Ma, my sides hurt so bad and I don't get a good sleep without waking up coughing."* If I could have gone through it for her, I would have. Instead, I did the best I could raising my four little grandchildren. On December 23, 1893, almost to the day her mother, Mary Ann, had died, Maggie Sage Glanville breathed her last breath. She left behind her husband, William, and four children, ages nine, eight, six, and three.

I probably was the only one that wasn't disappointed when the railroad chose Harveyville over Dover to extend its line and put in a new depot. The town folks fought valiantly to get it to come through Dover. I'm just not as young as I used to be, and I tire more easily. My nieces come and help me with the Inn, and we do OK, because business just isn't what it once was. Had the depot been built here, I'm sure it would all be different. But raising four little ones again—and taking care of what guests we do have, is more than enough for me. I now have seven granddaughters, as James and Lizzie had Mabel, Beryl and Jessie after Maggie died.

I asked Alfred how he could wind up with all these little girls running in and out, after coming from a male dominated Sage clan? Our only grandson, Oscar, is now 15 years old and able to help around this big place, but that's the only boy,

<u>so</u> <u>far.</u> Bill and Squire have started courting sisters, Caroline and Eliza Sage, so who knows? [Caroline and Eliza are either unrelated to this Sage family or distant cousins. Could not find descendants of Bill and Caroline. Squire and Eliza descendants are Ada, Alfred and Mamie. Thomas *"Dudley"* and Amelia *"Minnie"* Kelly descendants are Clarence and Thomas Paul.]

For the past few days, I've been feeling a tightness in my chest. At first I dismissed it as indigestion, or even illness when it lasted more than one day, but now I'm concerned that it could be more than that. After all, I'm 81 years old, but like my mother, I've never really been sick a day in my life.

On March 28, 1899, I awoke in the night with a sharp pain and shortness of breath. I knew this big heart may be breaking, because when it's your time, it's your time. Well, I thought to myself, it's almost a new century. I leaned over and touched the soft bearded face that was the last thing I saw before going to sleep these past 35 years.

Alfred stirred, *"You, ok, Mary Ann?"*

"I'm fine, go back to sleep."

Then I whispered softly, *"I love you."*

Alfred whispered back, *"I love you too. Goodnight Mary Ann."*

Epilogue

Alfred Sage lived five years into the new century (1905); five years, which were the first in over 45 years without a Mary Ann at his side. He continued doing business in Dover until his death. He operated the Sage Inn and Somerset Hall across from the Inn. The Odd Fellows, including Alfred Sage, began their fraternal brotherhood upstairs in this store. Aaron Sage and his two sons, George and Fred, fiddled for dances on Saturday nights on the top floor of Somerset Hall. The building became the heartbeat of the community, and continues to be to this day. Most folks referred to it as simply "Sage Hall." Alfred never missed a dance, choosing to sit in a chair, often with his eyes closed, smiling, and remembering.

Did Alfred Sage love either Mary Ann Bassett or Mary Ann Buell more than the other? From what I've been able to tell, he loved them both—differently. Mary Ann Bassett was his wife for only nine years, but she had been his one and only sweetheart. He grew up with her. She had actually been a part of his life for much, much longer. They had five children together, in a short time; a testament to their strong desire for each other. I think he always loved her.

Mary Ann Buell was a strong, dynamic woman. She complemented Alfred's drive for success. Indeed, she was instrumental in the success he achieved. She found room in her heart for not only Alfred, but five little children. While "romance" may not have been what brought them together, they needed each other. She was Alfred's rock, and he, hers. In many ways, they were more aligned in their thinking than he and Mary Ann Bassett. The fact that Alfred's heirs chose to have him buried beside Mary Ann Buell in the Dover cemetery speaks loudly about the love they perceived their father had for her.

Alfred Sage died at the age of 71 after being ill with gastritis for about two weeks. At 4 in the morning on April 17, 1905, Dr. Charles Bradley was raised by an urgent knocking at his door. He was asked to come quickly. Dr. Bradley worked faithfully to save his life but at 7 a.m. he was pronounced dead. His funeral was held two days later at the Sage Inn. The local newspapers remembered Alfred Sage in this way:

"No man could have a better friend than he, no worthy man, however poor, ever went to him for a favor that he did not get it. He was kindhearted to an extreme degree and sympathetic, hospitable, the sorrows and misfortunes of his fellow men troubled him deeply and brought forth a ready and generous response. He was plain, without deceit or pretensions. Alf Sage will certainly be rewarded in the life to come. He accumulated much of the worlds goods and the affections of all who knew him."

My husband, Michael, and I moved to the Sage Inn in May, 2001. I was like a sponge, soaking up as much information about the history of the Inn and the Dover/Mission Creek area as I could. For over two years, I collected stories from the locals and made trips to the Topeka & Shawnee County Library, the Wabaunsee County Museum, and the Kansas State Historical Research Center. Wayne Gurtler of Dover, who had inherited the Sage Inn and the surrounding land, allowed me to study abstracts going back to military bounty land warrants. I interviewed as many members of the Sage family, still living in this area, as I could.

Fortunately, the Dover community has always taken an interest in its history. Vey Bassett Rutledge Spaulding's book, *Dover Then and Now*, was published in 1964. The Dover Heritage Day Association had the foresight to undertake the publication of a series of booklets with early historical facts, and I used these to check against my own research. Since the new millennium, the Dover Community Foundation has made two videos on Dover's early history and country schools under the guidance of Ellen Sage Randall. I knew I didn't want to replicate the efforts of others. In writing, *Goodnight, Mary Ann*, my focus was on the "story" behind the first Sage family. If other Dover ancestors were here during that time period, I tried to include information about them as well, but not everyone's family is mentioned.

History is remembered best when told as a story. I wanted to give our guests at the Sage Inn a memorable story about this wonderfully unique place. *Goodnight, Mary Ann* is one part fact, one part lore, and one part inspiration (i.e. Mary Ann Sage was a strong abolitionist—obituary fact; the Sage's were involved in the underground railroad—lore; *"I could not live with myself if I did not aid those slaves…"*—inspiration). There's some good history in these pages; but there's also tales that served as bridges to get me from one piece of historical fact to another. It took me much longer to write than I had anticipated because I tried to "weave" together bits and pieces from other sources and two file folders full of scraps of paper and old newspaper clippings.

Finally, I would be remiss if I didn't mention that the writings of Topeka authors, Tom Goodrich and Roy Bird, were essential to my being able to ground the story in the Kansas Territorial—Civil War era.

Goodnight, Mary Ann was fun to write. After a day of zoning at the keyboard, Mike and I would hop in the pick up and start prowling the back roads of Shawnee and Wabaunsee Counties. I'd tell him that if my suspicions were right, we should find the remains of an old stone house right about…here. Wow, the adrenaline rush when we'd actually find the old remains of a house or stone bridge! The book may have started out to be something to market at the bed and breakfast, but I think it wound up meaning much more. It is my gift to the people of Dover. Long after I am gone, I hope Dover grandchildren and great-grandchildren will cherish it.

I must confess to you, the reader, that what brought about a book, entitled, *Goodnight Mary Ann*, was the presence of an unidentifiable noise in one of our guest rooms. We never talked about this with others for fear that they'd think we were making it up, or that it would be bad for business. We had only lived at the Sage Inn a month when a guest reported a sw-ish-ing sound in the night that she could only relate to sounding like an old steam engine, like a train waiting at a station for departure. She even went so far as to ask some of the locals if there was some type of pumping station close by that operated only in the night. She was told that as far as anyone knew, there hadn't been a steam engine around here since the old saw/grist mill was operating.

Then there was the woman who felt very cold and felt a cool breeze on her face, despite her husband sleeping without covers next to her, who hadn't felt anything. In fact, at one point she was so cold her teeth chattered!

Next we had guests show up at the breakfast table and inquire about who had come to the inn in the middle of the night. *"Surely, you all heard it, they knocked and knocked like it was something urgent."* Now, Mike and I are really starting to wonder about things.

There's more. The next inquiry was about someone digging. *"Digging?"*

"Yes, you could hear the shovel going in and being drug across the dirt. Sounded like someone was digging a well...or a grave!" Those guests even hunted around the perimeter of the Inn to see if someone was trying to play a joke on them.

Still another time, it was scratching, like an animal trapped and scratching at wood trying to get out...or in!

Or another, it would be sawing, like there were workers sawing outside.

Or another, sounded like furniture being moved.

Mind you, these incidents have happened with enough frequency, and with so many different people, that we don't know what to make of it. The one that took the cake, however, was the middle-age woman who was sharing a room with her sister. Right before dawn, she felt like she was short on oxygen and couldn't get air. She opened her eyes to see the vision of a woman, hair tied back, wearing a long cape, hovering over her. This woman was not story telling to have something to share at breakfast! In fact, she waited until everyone else had left the breakfast table to talk to me in private. I knew something was wrong immediately because as she began to tell me what happened, her face went pale and she had goosebumps on her arms. She told me she was frozen in fear, as she slid her hand over to shake her sister awake. When her sister did awake, the vision vanished. She asked me if I believed her. After all the other things that had happened, I said, *"Yes."*

The very next day, I was determined to get a copy of Mary Ann Buell Sage's obituary, hoping that it may provide some answers. Well, it did provide many answers really, but not about all of this. Mary Ann's maiden name had been incorrectly printed in past information. In fact, until I got a copy of the obituary, I did not know that she was the mother of two sons by the last name of Dennitt. What's more, I did not know that she was the daughter of Elizabeth Jones Sayer. I recognized both the Dennitt and Sayer names from old abstracts. And so, the sleuthing began.

The Sage family was a difficult family to ferret out because there were so many of them, and so many of their children named by the same names. It didn't help that Grandpa Samuel had two sets of children by two different wives, either! But, I'm glad I put forth the effort. One of the stories that I have heard from several locals was that the Sage's never went to church. That may have been true for some of the clan, but I hope you will realize after reading this that Alfred and Mary Ann were charter members of the Baptist Church. Mary Ann started the first organized worship services in Dover. I found reference to Alfred being at the baptism of the Wirths. At one point Alfred conveyed part of his land to build a parish for the Baptist Church. [This may be the home at 13543 SW K-4 Highway.] That doesn't exactly sound like the actions of a non-Christian.

As far as noises, and things that go bump in the night? Well the only thing that Mike and I have heard is the screen door on the Inn opening and closing. It drags on the threshold's stone slab. We can be sitting in the parlor and sometimes the door opens, then closes. No matter how quickly we run to check it out, there will not be a sign of anyone being around. Perhaps these sounds can be explained by the events that have taken place over the past 138 years. Perhaps Mary Ann Dennitt Buell Sage is still looking after guests. It troubles me greatly, however, that I was never able to find out where Mary Ann Bassett Sage was buried. Perhaps, she, too, wanted to share Alfred's life at the Historic Sage Inn.

Genealogy

Samuel Sage 4/6/1775–12/9/1871
  First wife—Sharlot Hayden, Family lived in England
    Children—
    Charlotte [1815–?]
    George [1816–1856]
    Aaron [1819–1839]
    Mary Hannah [1820–?]

    George Sage married Mary Guppy. Moved to NY in 1847. Their children were:
        Charlotte Sage Guest [1840–1908] (NY)
        Henry Valentine Sage [1843–1892] (KS)
        Eliza Ellen Sage [1847–1858] (NY)
        John William Sage [1851–1933] (KS)
        Hannah Sage Doane [1859–1925] (NY)

Samuel Sage's
Second Wife—Elizabeth Davis, Family moved to America
Children—
Arthur [1826–1902]
Ann [1828–1885]
John [1830–1899]
Alfred [1833–1905]
Mark [1836–1919]
Samuel Jr. [1839–1864] (died during Civil War)
Aaron [1841–1942]
Elizabeth [1844–1921]
Walter [1845–1861] (died during Civil War)

Arthur Sage married Keziah Sheppard. Their children were:
Albert
Ann
Sarah
Emily
Henry (died as infant)

Ann Sage married Simon Main. Their children were:
Johnny (died as infant)
Morris
Hester
Frank
Joe
Ellen
Alfred
Libby
Addie
Albert

John Sage married Elizabeth Bassett. Their children were:
Emma
Samuel
Maddie
Mack
Edwin
Charley
Earl

Alfred Sage married Mary Ann Bassett. Their children were:
William "Bill"
Squire
James
Margaret "Maggie"
Thomas "Dud"

Mark Sage married Josephine Howe. Their children were:
Frank Howe
Jennie
Ida
Rose
Walter
Mark "Arc"
Will
Edgar
Tom

Aaron Sage married Eliza Smith Dennitt. Their children were:
George
William (died as infant)
Fred
Clark
Minnie
Charlie

Elizabeth Sage married Ed Stock. Their children were:
Frank
Mattie

Bibliography

Alma Enterprise, 1899.

Ancestry.com at the Topeka and Shawnee County Public Library.

Bird, Roy: <u>They Deserved a Better Fate, The Second Kansas State Militia and the Price Raid 1864</u>, Cummings & Hathaway Publishers, NY, 1999.

Castel, Albert: <u>Civil War Times</u>, 1940.

Chinn, Stephen: *UKan Heritage Server*, Vanderbilt University.

Church of Jesus Christ of Latter-Day Saints, *FamilySearch.Org.*

Cone, William: <u>Historical Sketch of Shawnee County</u>, 1877.

Connelley, William E.: <u>Kansas and Kansans</u>, Lewis Publishing Company, NY 1918.

Current, R. N., T. H. Williams, F. Freidel: <u>American History, A Survey,</u> 2nd Ed., Alfred A. Knopf Publisher, 1967.

Cutler, William G.: <u>History of Kansas</u>, A. T. Andreas Publisher, Chicago, IL, 1883.

Dover Heritage Day Association, <u>Dover Heritage Books</u>, 5 Volume Set, 1987-1992.

Enterprise Chronicle, Feb. 5, 1976.

Emporia News, 1868/1869.

Eskridge Star, December, 1893.

Giles, Frye W.: <u>Historical Sketch of Shawnee County</u>, 1876.

Goodrich, Thomas, War to the Knife, Stackpole Books, Mechanicsburg, PA, 1998.

Historical Album of Kansas, Garvey Foundation, 1961.

Jordan, Robert Paul: The Civil War, National Geographic Society, 1969.

Kansas Historical Quarterlys: Kansas State Historical Society.

Kansas State Historical Society: Life of Lane, 1930.

Kansas State Historical Society: *Shawnee County Clippings,* 1861-1882.

Kansas State Record, 1859.

King, James L.: Historical Sketch of Shawnee County, 1905.

Lawrence Herald of Freedom, 1855.

Lilburn, Michelle: Kaw Nation of Oklahoma Tribal Office.

Long, Howard: *Flint Hills Independent,* March 25, 1993.

McAllaster, O.W.: *My Experience in the Lawrence Raid,* Skyways Library.

McCutcheon, Marc: Everyday Life in the 1800's—A Guide for Writers, Students and Historians, Writers Digest Books, Cincinnati, OH, 2001.

McHenry, Andrew: Family History, Maple Hill.

Morris, Werner: Pioneer Trails from U.S. Land Surveys, 1988, Rev. 1995.

Pennsylvania—Numerous Reference Books in the Geneology Section of the Topeka and Shawnee County Public Library.

Pratt, Fletcher: Civil War in Pictures, Garden City Books, Garden City, NY, 1955.

Prentis, Noble L.: History of Kansas, Caroline Prentis, publisher, 1909.

Shawnee County Historical Society: Bulletin 22, December, 1954.

Shawnee County Register of Deeds, 1855-1858.

Skyways.lib.ks.us/genweb/shawnee/library/1878

Spaulding, Vey Bassett Rutledge: <u>Dover Then and Now</u>, Phelps Creative Printing, 1964.

Stubbs, Michael: *Communique on Underground Railroad,* May, 2002.

Tabor, Milton: <u>This Day in Kansas History</u>, 1954.

Territorial Kansas Heritage Alliance: *John Brown of Kansas 1855-1859,* May, 2001.

Topeka State Journal: 75th Anniversary, 1854-1929.

United States Census, 1850/1855.

Wabaunsee County Historical Society: <u>Early History of Wabaunsee County</u>, 1901.

Wabaunsee County Historical Society: <u>New Branches from Old Trees, a History of Wabaunsee County</u>, 1976.

Wallace, Douglass W. and Roy D. Bird: <u>Witness of the Times</u>; Shawnee County Historical Society & Shawnee County American Revolution Bicentennial Committee, July 4, 1976.

Recipes

from the

H I S T O R I C

1878 SAGE INN

& Stage Coach Station

National Register of Historic Places

BED AND BREAKFAST (LLC)

Mike & Debra Stufflebean, Innkeepers

13553 SW K-4 Highway

Dover, KS 66420

www.historicsageinn.com

1-866-INN-OPEN

Kansas Bed & Breakfast Association

Apple Pancakes w/Cider Syrup (Serves 4)

Pancake Batter

1 c flour
1 T sugar
1 1/2 tsp baking powder
1/2 tsp salt
1/4 tsp cinnamon
1 c applesauce
1/4 tsp vanilla
2 eggs
1 T butter

Whisk ingredients together and let set. Spray griddle with cooking spray.

Cider Syrup

2 c apple cider
1 1/2 c brown sugar
1 cinnamon stick
1 1/2 tsp whole cloves

Bring to boil and cook over medium heat until liquid is reduced to desired syrup consistency. Remove spices with strainer.

Whole Grain Pecan Pancakes (Serves 4)

1 c whole wheat flour
1/2 c rolled oats
1 tsp baking powder
1/2 tsp cinnamon
1/4 tsp nutmeg
1 1/2 c milk
1 egg
2 T vegetable oil
2 T honey
1 grated apple
(or 2 individual-helping packaged applesauce)
1/4 c pecans
1/4 c sunflower meats

Mix dry ingredients in separate mixing bowl. Mix remaining ingredients together and add to dry. Cook on oiled griddle.

French Toast (Serves 4)

2 eggs
1/4 c milk
1 tsp vanilla
1/2 tsp cinnamon
1/2 tsp nutmeg
1/3 c Bisquick
4 thick slices of bread

Beat together with whisk. Dip bread into batter. Place in skillet of hot oil and fry on both sides.

Over-night French Toast (Serves 8)

Chunks of Bread
8 oz pkg cream cheese
10 eggs
2 c milk
1/3 c maple syrup

Tear enough bread into chunks to fill a 13" x 9" greased cake pan. Take a spoon and put pieces of cream cheese throughout the bread. Whisk or beat eggs with milk, add syrup. Pour over bread and cheese. Cover with plastic wrap and let sit in refrigerator over night. Remove wrap to bake in 375 deg oven for about one hour. Put a knife in the middle to be sure the eggs are done in center. Top with Praline Syrup. You can vary this recipe by also mixing coconut, pecans or raisins with the chunks of bread.

Praline Syrup

1 stick butter
2 c brown sugar
1 cup pecans (optional)

Melt butter in saucepan, add brown sugar and enough water to blend with a wire whisk. Bring to a low boil. Stay with the syrup as it can become volatile if not stirred. Will thicken as it cools.

Stuffed Waffles

Waffle Mix (Serves 8)

3 c flour
2 1/2 tsp baking powder
1/4 tsp baking soda
4 T melted butter
1/2 tsp salt
4 eggs
2 c buttermilk

Mix until Smooth—use Belgian Waffle Iron.

Filling

1 med onion chopped
2 mild banana peppers chopped
1 # ground sausage
1 c shredded cheddar cheese
1/2 c cottage cheese

Cook sausage with onion and peppers, drain grease. Add cheeses. Assemble with waffle halves like a sandwich. Top with Hollandaise sauce. Filling variation: Cream Cheese, 1 tsp orange extract, and orange marmalaid blended together. Top with maple syrup.

Hollandaise Sauce

2 eggs
6 T lemon juice
1/2 tsp salt
2 sticks melted butter

Melt butter in saucepan. Whisk eggs, lemon juice and salt together. Pour into melted butter and whisk over low heat until thickened.

Eggs Benedict

Eggs
Butter
English Muffins
Sliced Ham

Using a poaching pan fill w/water to bottom of egg cups. Bring to a boil. Put 1/2 tsp butter in cups; let melt and fill with egg. Cook until egg is set (white is firm but yolk is soft). Serve on toasted English muffin, with ham, then egg. Top with Hollandaise sauce and sprinkle with Paprika.

Pumpkin Nut Waffles (Serves 6–8)

3 eggs, separated
1 tsp cream of tarter
1 3/4 c milk
1/2 vegetable oil
1/2 c canned pumpkin
2 1/2 c flour
4 tsp baking powder

1 tsp salt
3/4 tsp cinnamon
1/4 tsp nutmeg
3/4 c chopped pecans

Beat 3 egg whites with 1 tsp cream of tarter until stiff; set aside. Whisk together remaining ingredients in large mixing bowl, folding in pecans and egg whites right before baking in hot waffle iron.

Walnut Syrup

2 C maple syrup
1/2 C honey
1 T cinnamon
1/2 tsp ground cloves
1 C chopped English Walnuts

Microwave ingredients together until hot, stir with small whisk.

Bacon & Cheese Waffles (serves 4)

1 egg
1 1/4 C milk
1 C (8 oz) sour cream
1 T melted butter
2 C Bisquick
1 tsp baking powder
6–8 strips of fried bacon, crumbled
1 C shredded cheddar cheese

Whisk together ingredients in order given, folding in the crumbled bacon and cheese right before ready to put into hot waffle iron.

Sage Frittata (serves 4)

6 garden green onions
1 T olive oil
20 cherry tomatoes
7 sage leaves
8 eggs
1/2 tsp Kosher salt
1/4 tsp pepper
1/2 c shredded colby or cheddar cheese

Preheat broiler. Sautee in 12" iron skillet
six chopped onion bulbs in olive oil. Whisk 8 eggs, add salt, pepper, and finally
chopped sage leaves. Pour over onions in skillet. Continue to cook, moving edges
so runny top part of omelet can seep under and cook. Once eggs have set, cover
with halved cherry tomatoes, chopped onion greens, and shredded cheese. Put
skillet under broiler until top is lightly browned. Loosen with spatula and transfer
to platter.

Old-Fashioned Baked Eggs
(Serves 8–10)

14–16 eggs
1 c half & half
1 T chives
3/4 c sour cream
2 T butter
salt & pepper
2 c chopped ham
1 1/2 c shredded cheddar cheese

Whisk eggs with all other ingredients, except meat and cheese. Pour into buttered 13" x 9" pan. Distribute ham and cheese by placing into the egg mixture after it is poured in the baking dish. Bake at 350 deg for 45 minutes to 1 hour, when knife inserted comes out clean. Try these different variations: fry 1# of spicey ground sausage for the meat (drain well, blot with paper towel, and dust with flour); use Swiss or Monterey Jack for the cheese; add diced sweet peppers; add diced mushrooms; add diced green onions; 5 minutes before eggs are done baking, remove from oven and top with bread cubes, pour 1 stick melted butter over bread, return to oven on broil until croutons are crispy; top eggs with Hollandaise sauce; top eggs with salsa and a dollop of sour cream.

Kanza Quiche (Serves 6)

9" pie shell
15.5 oz can golden hominey
3 eggs
3/4 c evap milk (or cream)
2–2.5 oz jars dried beef
1 T basil
1 tsp garlic powder
1 c shredded Colby cheese
salt & pepper

Tine unbaked pie shell (if frozen, let thaw first). Bake 10 minutes at 375 deg. Drain canned hominey and put in bottom of baked shell. Whisk together eggs and milk. Add seasoning and pour over hominey. Shred dried beef into egg mixture. Top with shredded cheese. Bake another 30 minutes.

Hashbrown Quiche (Serves 6)

12 oz shredded hashbrowns, thawed
1/4 c melted butter
1 c shredded Cheddar cheese
1 c shredded Swiss cheese
1 c diced ham
3/4 c milk
3 eggs
salt & pepper

Grease a 9" pie plate. Blot hashbrowns with paper towel before placing in bottom of pie plate. Pack hashbrowns to form crust. Brush with melted butter. Bake at 425 deg for 25 minutes. Remove from oven. Layer cheeses and ham on top of crust. Whisk milk, eggs, salt & pepper together and pour over contents. Reduce oven to 350 deg and bake another 25 minutes.

Herb Cheese Quiche (Serves 6)

1 unbaked 9" pie shell
2 med onions, chopped
2 T butter
1 c Cheddar (or Colby) cheese
3 eggs, beaten
salt
1 1/2 T flour
1 can cream of celery soup
1/2 c milk
1/2 tsp thyme
1/2 tsp basil

Saute onions in butter and spread in bottom of pie crust. Sprinkle cheese over onions. Blend remaining ingredients in mixing bowl and pour over onions and cheese. Bake at 350 deg for 45 minutes.

Lemon Souffle`

2 T softened butter
3/4 c sugar
2 egg yolks
1 lemon, juice & rind
2 T flour
1 c milk
2 egg whites

Beat egg whites until stiff in separate bowl. Cream together butter, sugar and egg yolks. Add lemon juice and zest, flour, and milk. Fold egg whites into mixture, whisking only until blended. Bake in a greased 5 1/2" round souffle`baking dish at 325 deg for 45 minutes. Don't open and close oven door during baking.

Cheese Souffle` (Serves 6)

Butter
Grated Parmesan Cheese
2 T butter
4 T flour
1 c half & half
1/2 tsp salt
1/8 tsp nutmeg
1/8 tsp white pepper
5 jumbo egg yolks
1/2 c shredded Parmesan cheese
6 jumbo egg whites, room temp.
1/4 tsp cream of tartar
red and yellow food coloring

Coat 6 individual souffle` dishes with butter. Sprinkle bottoms with Parmesan cheese. In saucepan, melt butter, stir in flour. Cook the flour, then add half & half and seasonings, and continue cooking until thickens. In bowl, beat egg yolks with whisk. Stir in some of the hot sauce into yolks and whisk. Add egg mixture to sauce. Stir in cheese. Cover. [This part can be made several hours ahead of time. Simply reheat to lukewarm when ready to resume.] Beat egg whites with cream of tartar until stiff. Add enough food coloring to match the color of the egg sauce. Whisk about 1 c of egg whites into sauce until smooth. Fold in remaining egg whites. Pour into individual souffle` dishes and bake for 40–45 minutes at 350 deg.

Coffee Cake

1 yellow butter cake mix
2 eggs
2/3 c warm water
2 pkgs instant dry yeast
1 c flour
21 oz can pie filling
5 T melted butter
1 c powdered sugar
1 T water
1 T corn syrup

Mix 1 1/2 c cake mix with eggs, water, yeast and flour. Beat 2 minutes. Spead into 13" x 9" greased cakepan. Top with pie filling. Melt butter in microwave and add to remaining cake mix, and enough flour to make crumbly struesel topping. Bake at 375 deg for 30–40 minutes (when center is nolonger gooey). Microwave powder sugar, water and corn syrup and drizzle over warm cake.

Lemon Breakfast Cake

1 lemon cake mix
eggs, oil, etc. according to mix directions
2 small boxes lemon jello
1 T melted butter
1 c powdered sugar
1 T water

Mix cake mix according to package directions, but also add two boxes of dry lemon jello. Bake according to box instructions. When cake is warm, punch holes in it with a meat fork. Whisk together butter, sugar and water. Pour over cake. Let cake cool and absorb liquid.

Apple Cake

2 c peeled Golden Delicious apples
1 c sugar
1 egg
1/4 tsp salt
1 1/2 tsp cinnamon
1 tsp baking soda
1 c flour
1/2 c chopped English Walnuts
Sauce: 1/4 c brown sugar
1/4 c sugar
1 tsp flour
2 T butter
1/2 tsp vanilla extract
1/2 c water

Prepare apples and toss with sugar. Whisk egg with remaining ingredients to make thick batter. Add to apples. Pour batter into greased 9" x 9" baking dish. Bake at 350 deg for 40 minutes. Bring ingredients for sauce to boil in saucepan. Boil for 2 minutes, stirring. When cake comes out of oven, pour sauce over it to be absorbed.

Sticky Buns

20 frozen bread dough balls
1 stick melted butter
1 pkg vanilla pudding
1/2 c brown sugar
2 T cinnamon
1/2 c chopped pecans or raisins

Put frozen dough balls in a well-greased 9" x 13" baking dish. Melt butter in microwave and pour over balls. Sprinkle remaining ingredients over moistened balls. Cover with wax paper that has been sprayed with cookie spray. Let set in cold oven over night. Remove wax paper. Preheat oven to 350 deg. Bake 25 to 30 minutes. Invert immediately on wax paper to cool. Variation: Use lemon pudding, 1/2 c powdered sugar, 2 tsp cardamom.

Sage & Raisin Scones

3 c flour
1/4 c sugar
2 1/2 tsp baking powder
1/4 tsp baking soda
1/4 tsp salt
1/8 c minced fresh sage leaves
12 T butter
1 c buttermilk
2/3 c raisins
1 T milk
1 tsp cinnamon
3 T powdered sugar

Combine all dry ingredients with sage. Cut in pieces of the butter with pastry blender to form coarse meal. With a fork, stir in buttermilk. Knead dough on floured bread board to knead in raisins. Roll dough into 1/2" thick rectangle. Cut 8–10 scones with biscuit cutter. Place on sprayed baking sheet 1" apart. Bake at 375 deg for 10 minutes. Combine milk, cinnamon and powdered sugar. Brush on scones and bake another 5 minutes until golden on top.

Strawberry Scones

4 c flour
2 T sugar
2 T baking powder
2 tsp Kosher salt
3 sticks of butter
5 eggs
1 c heavy whipping cream
1 c sliced fresh strawberries

Combine all dry ingredients and cut in pieces of the butter with pastry blender to form coarse meal. Whisk 4 eggs with cream and add to dry ingredients. Add strawberries. Knead dough on floured bread board to knead in berries. Roll dough into 1/2" thick rectangle. Cut 10–12 scones with biscuit cutter. Place on sprayed baking sheet 1" apart. Bake at 375 deg for 10 minutes. Whisk together 1 T water with 1 beaten egg. Brush on top of scones and sprinkle with sugar. Return to oven for 5 minutes until golden on top.

Irish Oatmeal Scones

2 1/4 c flour
1 c old-fashioned oatmeal
1 T baking powder
1/2 tsp baking soda
1/2 tsp salt
3/4 stick butter
1 large egg
3/4 c heavy whipping cream
4 T brown sugar
1 tsp vanilla extract
1/2 c golden raisins

Combine all dry ingredients and cut in pieces of the butter with pastry blender to form coarse meal. Whisk egg with brown sugar, cream and vanilla. Add to dry ingredients. Add raisins. Knead dough on floured bread board to knead in raisins. Roll dough into 1/2" thick rectangle. Cut 10–12 scones with biscuit cutter. Place on sprayed baking sheet 1" apart. Bake at 400 deg for 15 minutes.

Breakfast Bread

3 c flour
2 tsp baking soda
1/2 tsp baking powder
1 1/2 tsp cinnamon
1 tsp salt
1/2 c chopped nuts (optional)
4 eggs
2 1/2 c sugar
1 c canola oil
2 tsp vanilla
Pumpkin Bread: 1 c water & 1–16 oz can (or 2 c) pumpkin & 1 tsp cloves
Zucchini Bread: 1–8 oz can crushed pineapple & 2 c shredded zucchini

Combine dry ingredients in separate bowl. Beat together eggs, sugar, oil and vanilla. Fold in either water, pumpkin and cloves to make 3 loaves of pumpkin bread, or fold in pineapple and zucchini to make zucchini bread. Bake in three greased bread loaf pans, dusted with flour, for 1 hour at 350 deg. Let cool 10 minutes in pan, invert.

0-595-29476-6